ARE YOU
READY
FOR SOME
FOOTBALL?

⊢—2019—⊣

ARE YOU
READY
FOR SOME
FOOTBALL?

Your Pocket Guide to the
2019 National Football League Season

By M. G. Ross

Are You Ready for Some Football?
Your Pocket Guide to the 2019 National Football League Season
By M. G. Ross

Library of Congress Cataloging-In-Publication Data
Ross, M.G.
Are You Ready for Some Football?/ M.G. Ross
ISBN 978-1073498376

Cover Design by Amber Colleran

For more information or to contact the author, send emails to
MGRoss.Football@gmail.com

This book is dedicated to my father and grandfather, who inspired in me a love of football, a love of hard work and fair play, and an unapologetic belief in keeping score.

Special thanks go to my incomparable designer, Sekayi Stephens, who turned my pen scratchings into what you hold in your hands today, and my cover designer, Amber Colleran, who made sure my crazy idea looks like a real book.

TABLE OF CONTENTS

Introduction

faithful readers of this series know, when I decided to create an annual otball guide, I did it out of frustration. Having loved football since ildhood, I listen to sports talk radio religiously, am addicted to the NFL annel, spend way too much money on NFL Sunday Ticket so I can see ery game every week, and count the days between Super Bowl Sunday d the start of the pre-season. Like many of you, I watch the combine and e draft (you gotta love how the NFL has turned those into TV events!), d I spend lots of time on ESPN.com and NFL.com, tracking which free ents have signed with new teams, how the draft picks are shaping up, e latest player to have torn his ACL, and the revolving door of coaches d players.

But there was one thing I needed that I just couldn't find: a convenient, rtable, fan-friendly guide to the weekly schedule of games. Sure, you n see the schedule every week on line, but I wanted something I could ve in print, that I could write on and keep notes on and keep track of, ek after week. I could find team schedules for the year, but not a handy ll-year schedule that I could print out and use.

So, I decided to make one. As I worked on it, I included what I would ant, as the prototypical football fan. An easy to read week-by-week hedule. An at-a-glance schedule for each team. Room to keep track of ur picks and the final scores. A way to keep track of a team's record roughout the season. A little write-up on each team, including their head ach and their first-round draft pick, plus a reminder of how last season ded and what they've done in the offseason to get ready for this year. d a play-off section, where you can fill in your bracket as the play-offs e about to start, and then track each game throughout the postseason.

That's what you now hold in your hands. I hope you find it useful, I pe it makes watching football each week even more fun. And I hope you ll let me know if there are any improvements or additions you'd like me include in next year's edition.

Thanks for your support, and ... hey... it's almost time for kick-off. Gotta go.

M.G.Ross
July 2019
MGRoss.Football@gmail.com

How to Use This Book

a football fan, you have a pretty good idea of which teams are strong,
ich teams face a "challenge" and which teams are poised for a break-
t. But every season has its share of surprises and disappointments.

This pocket guide is designed to make it fun to watch the games
ch week, and easy to keep track of your favorite teams and the whole
gue as the season marches on.

The very first thing I want you to do is to **turn to page 5** and fill out
ur 2019 Season Predictions. This is highly speculative, of course — but
your chance to say, at the very start of the season, who you think will
the winners when it's all over in December. As a reminder, on **page 4**
u'll see all the **NFL Teams by Division and Conference**.

As the regular season starts, the **Weekly Schedules** are your chance
handicap the games in advance, and predict who will win and who will
e each week. I suggest that every Thursday, before the first game of
e week starts, you fill out your weekly predictions for that week. Use the
eekly Schedules section (page 7) to make your picks, and to keep track of
w well you do. At the end of the week (after Monday night's game) tally up
ur predictions and enter your "score" for the week on the **Scorecard** sheet
age 90). Use this sheet to keep track of your wins and losses each week
ring the regular season. One note: all game times listed are in Eastern Time.

Most of us have a favorite team (and some of us have a team we love to
te) — use the **Team Schedules** (page 25) to keep track of how each team
doing, especially in those all-important divisional match-ups. As the end
the season approaches, you will have a birds-eye view of how the playoffs
e shaping up and who is likely to make it to the post-season.

Once the regular season is over, use the **Playoffs** section to make
atching the post-season fun. First thing you want to do is to compare
ose predictions you made at the beginning of the season (back on page
with the actual results (fill in your **Division Winners** Sheet, page 93).
en it's time to fill in your bracket: You know who the six teams are from
e NFC and the AFC — enter the teams into the bracket (on your **2019
ayoff Bracket Predictions**, page 96) , and then take a shot at predicting
o will make it through and wind up in the Super Bowl. Then follow along
the playoffs unfold, using your **2019 Playoff Bracket Tracker** (page 97)
keep track of who advances each week on the road to Super Bowl 52.

Finally, make sure to **order your 2020 guide** (p. 103) — and please
: me know if there is anything you'd like to add or change in next year's
lition by emailing me at MGRoss.Football@gmail.com. I look forward to
aring from you — and to a great *100ᵗʰ season* of the NFL.

NFL Teams By Division and Conference

NFC NORTH

Chicago Bears
Detroit Lions
Green Bay Packers
Minnesota Vikings

AFC NORTH

Baltimore Ravens
Cincinnati Bengals
Cleveland Browns
Pittsburgh Steelers

NFC SOUTH

Atlanta Falcons
Carolina Panthers
New Orleans Saints
Tampa Bay Buccaneers

AFC SOUTH

Houston Texans
Indianapolis Colts
Jacksonville Jaguars
Tennessee Titans

NFC EAST

Dallas Cowboys
New York Giants
Philadelphia Eagles
Washington Redskins

AFC EAST

Buffalo Bills
Miami Dolphins
New England Patriots
New York Jets

NFC WEST

Arizona Cardinals
Los Angeles Rams
San Francisco 49ers
Seattle Seahawks

AFC WEST

Denver Broncos
Kansas City Chiefs
Los Angeles Chargers
Oakland Raiders

Your 2019 Season Predictions

this in before the season even starts — can you predict who's going to
n each division — and who the wildcard teams will be?

C

vision Winners:

North _____

South _____

East _____

West _____

ild Card 1 _____

ild Card 2 _____

C

vision Winners:

North _____

South _____

East _____

West _____

ild Card 1 _____

ild Card 2 _____

WEEKLY SCHEDULES

WEEK 1: September 5-9

Pick your winners before the games start, then keep track of the scores as they happ

Thursday Night Game

☐ Green Bay Packers   ☐ at Chicago Bears   8:20 pm   ___
Final Score: _____ v. _____

Sunday Games

☐ Atlanta Falcons   ☐ at Minnesota Vikings   1 pm   ___
Final Score: _____ v. _____

☐ Buffalo Bills   ☐ at New York Jets   ___
Final Score: _____ v. _____

☐ Baltimore Ravens   ☐ at Miami Dolphins   ___
Final Score: _____ v. _____

☐ Kansas City Chiefs   ☐ at Jacksonville Jaguars   ___
Final Score: _____ v. _____

☐ Los Angeles Rams   ☐ at Carolina Panthers   ___
Final Score: _____ v. _____

☐ Tennessee Titans   ☐ at Cleveland Browns   ___
Final Score: _____ v. _____

☐ Washington Redskins   ☐ at Philadelphia Eagles   ___
Final Score: _____ v. _____

☐ Cincinnati Bengals   ☐ at Seattle Seahawks   4 pm   ___
Final Score: _____ v. _____

☐ Detroit Lions   ☐ at Arizona Cardinals   ___
Final Score: _____ v. _____

☐ Indianapolis Colts   ☐ at Los Angeles Chargers   ___
Final Score: _____ v. _____

☐ New York Giants   ☐ at Dallas Cowboys   ___
Final Score: _____ v. _____

☐ San Francisco 49ers   ☐ at Tampa Bay Buccaneers   ___
Final Score: _____ v. _____

Sunday Night Game

☐ Pittsburgh Steelers   ☐ at New England Patriots   8:20 pm   ___
Final Score: _____ v. _____

Monday Night Games

☐ Houston Texans   ☐ at New Orleans Saints   7:10 pm   ___
Final Score: _____ v. _____

☐ Denver Broncos   ☐ at Oakland Raiders   10:20 pm   ___
Final Score: _____ v. _____

WEEK 2: September 12-18

k your winners before the games start, then keep track of the scores as they happen.

			✓ **Your Correct Picks**
ursday Night Game			
☐ Tampa Bay Buccaneers	☐ at Carolina Panthers	8:20 pm	___
Final Score: ___ v. ___			
¹day Games			
☐ Arizona Cardinals	☐ at Baltimore Ravens	1 pm	___
Final Score: ___ v. ___			
☐ Buffalo Bills	☐ at New York Giants		___
Final Score: ___ v. ___			
☐ Dallas Cowboys	☐ at Washington Redskins		___
Final Score: ___ v. ___			
☐ Indianapolis Colts	☐ at Tennessee Titans		___
Final Score: ___ v. ___			
☐ Jacksonville Jaguars	☐ at Houston Texans		___
Final Score: ___ v. ___			
☐ Los Angeles Chargers	☐ at Detroit Lions		___
Final Score: ___ v. ___			
☐ Minnesota Vikings	☐ at Green Bay Packers		___
Final Score: ___ v. ___			
☐ New England Patriots	☐ at Miami Dolphins		___
Final Score: ___ v. ___			
☐ San Francisco 49ers	☐ at Cincinnati Bengals		___
Final Score: ___ v. ___			
☐ Seattle Seahawks	☐ at Pittsburgh Steelers		___
Final Score: ___ v. ___			
☐ Chicago Bears	☐ at Denver Broncos	4 pm	___
Final Score: ___ v. ___			
☐ Kansas City Chiefs	☐ at Oakland Raiders		___
Final Score: ___ v. ___			
☐ New Orleans Saints	☐ at Los Angeles Rams		___
Final Score: ___ v. ___			
nday Night Game			
☐ Philadelphia Eagles	☐ at Atlanta Falcons	8:20 pm	___
Final Score: ___ v. ___			
¹nday Night Game			
☐ Cleveland Browns	☐ at New York Jets	8:15 pm	___
Final Score: ___ v. ___			

WEEK 3: September 19-23

Pick your winners before the games start, then keep track of the scores as they happ

Thursday Night Game

✓ **Your**
Correct Pic

☐ Tennessee Titans ☐ at Jacksonville Jaguars 8:20 pm ____
Final Score: _____ v. _____

Sunday Games

☐ Atlanta Falcons ☐ at Indianapolis Colts 1 pm ____
Final Score: _____ v. _____

☐ Baltimore Ravens ☐ at Kansas City Chiefs ____
Final Score: _____ v. _____

☐ Cincinnati Bengals ☐ at Buffalo Bills ____
Final Score: _____ v. _____

☐ Denver Broncos ☐ at Green Bay Packers ____
Final Score: _____ v. _____

☐ Detroit Lions ☐ at Philadelphia Eagles ____
Final Score: _____ v. _____

☐ Miami Dolphins ☐ at Dallas Cowboys ____
Final Score: _____ v. _____

☐ New York Jets ☐ at New England Patriots ____
Final Score: _____ v. _____

☐ Oakland Raiders ☐ at Minnesota Vikings ____
Final Score: _____ v. _____

☐ Carolina Panthers ☐ at Arizona Cardinals 4 pm ____
Final Score: _____ v. _____

☐ Houston Texans ☐ at Los Angeles Chargers ____
Final Score: _____ v. _____

☐ New Orleans Saints ☐ at Seattle Seahawks ____
Final Score: _____ v. _____

☐ New York Giants ☐ at Tampa Bay Buccaneers ____
Final Score: _____ v. _____

☐ Pittsburgh Steelers ☐ at San Francisco 49ers ____
Final Score: _____ v. _____

Sunday Night Game

☐ Los Angeles Rams ☐ at Cleveland Browns 8:20 pm ____
Final Score: _____ v. _____

Monday Night Game

☐ Chicago Bears ☐ at Washington Redskins 8:15 pm ____
Final Score: _____ v. _____

WEEK 4: September 26-30

k your winners before the games start, then keep track of the scores as they happen.

ursday Night Game			✓ Your Correct Picks
☐ Philadelphia Eagles	☐ at Green Bay Packers	8:20 pm	___
Final Score: ___ v. ___			

nday Games

☐ Carolina Panthers	☐ at Houston Texans	1 pm	___
Final Score: ___ v. ___			
☐ Cleveland Browns	☐ at Baltimore Ravens		___
Final Score: ___ v. ___			
☐ Kansas City Chiefs	☐ at Detroit Lions		___
Final Score: ___ v. ___			
☐ Los Angeles Chargers	☐ at Miami Dolphins		___
Final Score: ___ v. ___			
☐ New England Patriots	☐ at Buffalo Bills		___
Final Score: ___ v. ___			
☐ Oakland Raiders	☐ at Indianapolis Colts		___
Final Score: ___ v. ___			
☐ Tennessee Titans	☐ at Atlanta Falcons		___
Final Score: ___ v. ___			
☐ Washington Redskins	☐ at New York Giants		___
Final Score: ___ v. ___			
☐ Jacksonville Jaguars	☐ at Denver Broncos	4 pm	___
Final Score: ___ v. ___			
☐ Minnesota Vikings	☐ at Chicago Bears		___
Final Score: ___ v. ___			
☐ Seattle Seahawks	☐ at Arizona Cardinals		___
Final Score: ___ v. ___			
☐ Tampa Bay Buccaneers	☐ at Los Angeles Rams		___
Final Score: ___ v. ___			

nday Night Game

☐ Dallas Cowboys	☐ at New Orleans Saints	8:20 pm	___
Final Score: ___ v. ___			

nday Night Game

☐ Cincinnati Bengals	☐ at Pittsburgh Steelers	8:15 pm	___
Final Score: ___ v. ___			

ams with bye: New York Jets, San Francisco 49ers

WEEK 5: October 3-7

Pick your winners before the games start, then keep track of the scores as they happen

Thursday Night Game

☐ Los Angeles Rams ☐ at Seattle Seahawks 8:20 pm ____
Final Score: _____ v. _____

Sunday Games

☐ Arizona Cardinals ☐ at Cincinnati Bengals 1 pm ____
Final Score: _____ v. _____

☐ Atlanta Falcons ☐ at Houston Texans ____
Final Score: _____ v. _____

☐ Baltimore Ravens ☐ at Pittsburgh Steelers ____
Final Score: _____ v. _____

☐ Buffalo Bills ☐ at Tennessee Titans ____
Final Score: _____ v. _____

☐ Chicago Bears ☐ at Oakland Raiders ____
Final Score: _____ v. _____

☐ Jacksonville Jaguars ☐ at Carolina Panthers ____
Final Score: _____ v. _____

☐ Minnesota Vikings ☐ at New York Giants ____
Final Score: _____ v. _____

☐ New England Patriots ☐ at Washington Redskins ____
Final Score: _____ v. _____

☐ New York Jets ☐ at Philadelphia Eagles ____
Final Score: _____ v. _____

☐ Tampa Bay Buccaneers ☐ at New Orleans Saints ____
Final Score: _____ v. _____

☐ Denver Broncos ☐ at Los Angeles Chargers 4 pm ____
Final Score: _____ v. _____

☐ Green Bay Packers ☐ at Dallas Cowboys ____
Final Score: _____ v. _____

Sunday Night Game

☐ Indianapolis Colts ☐ at Kansas City Chiefs 8:20 pm ____
Final Score: _____ v. _____

Monday Night Game

☐ Cleveland Browns ☐ at San Francisco 49ers 8:15 pm ____
Final Score: _____ v. _____

Teams with bye: Detroit Lions, Miami Dolphins

WEEK 6: October 10-14

k your winners before the games start, then keep track of the scores as they happen.

			✓ Your Correct Picks

ursday Night Game

☐ New York Giants ☐ at New England Patriots   8:20 pm   ____
Final Score: _____ v. _____

nday Games

☐ Carolina Panthers ☐ at Tampa Bay Buccaneers   9:30 am   ____
Final Score: _____ v. _____

☐ Cincinnati Bengals ☐ at Baltimore Ravens   1 pm   ____
Final Score: _____ v. _____

☐ Houston Texans ☐ at Kansas City Chiefs   ____
Final Score: _____ v. _____

☐ New Orleans Saints ☐ at Jacksonville Jaguars   ____
Final Score: _____ v. _____

☐ Philadelphia Eagles ☐ at Minnesota Vikings   ____
Final Score: _____ v. _____

☐ Seattle Seahawks ☐ at Cleveland Browns   ____
Final Score: _____ v. _____

☐ Washington Redskins ☐ at Miami Dolphins   ____
Final Score: _____ v. _____

☐ Atlanta Falcons ☐ at Arizona Cardinals   4 pm   ____
Final Score: _____ v. _____

☐ Dallas Cowboys ☐ at New York Jets   ____
Final Score: _____ v. _____

☐ San Francisco 49ers ☐ at Los Angeles Rams   ____
Final Score: _____ v. _____

☐ Tennessee Titans ☐ at Denver Broncos   ____
Final Score: _____ v. _____

unday Night Game

☐ Pittsburgh Steelers ☐ at Los Angeles Chargers   8:20 pm   ____
Final Score: _____ v. _____

onday Night Game

☐ Detroit Lions ☐ at Green Bay Packers   8:15 pm   ____
Final Score: _____ v. _____

eams with bye: Buffalo Bills, Chicago Bears, Indianapolis Colts, Oakland Raiders

13

WEEK 7: October 17-21

Pick your winners before the games start, then keep track of the scores as they happ

			✓ Your Correct Pic

Thursday Night Game

☐ Kansas City Chiefs ☐ at Denver Broncos 8:20 pm ___
Final Score: _____ v. _____

Sunday Games

☐ Arizona Cardinals ☐ at New York Giants 1 pm ___
Final Score: _____ v. _____

☐ Houston Texans ☐ at Indianapolis Colts ___
Final Score: _____ v. _____

☐ Jacksonville Jaguars ☐ at Cincinnati Bengals ___
Final Score: _____ v. _____

☐ Los Angeles Rams ☐ at Atlanta Falcons ___
Final Score: _____ v. _____

☐ Miami Dolphins ☐ at Buffalo Bills ___
Final Score: _____ v. _____

☐ Minnesota Vikings ☐ at Detroit Lions ___
Final Score: _____ v. _____

☐ Oakland Raiders ☐ at Green Bay Packers ___
Final Score: _____ v. _____

☐ San Francisco 49ers ☐ at Washington Redskins ___
Final Score: _____ v. _____

Baltimore Ravens ☐ at Seattle Seahawks 4 pm ___
Final Score: _____ v. _____

☐ Los Angeles Chargers ☐ at Tennessee Titans ___
Final Score: _____ v. _____

☐ New Orleans Saints ☐ at Chicago Bears ___
Final Score: _____ v. _____

Sunday Night Game

☐ Philadelphia Eagles ☐ at Dallas Cowboys 8:20 pm ___
Final Score: _____ v. _____

Monday Night Game

☐ New England Patriots ☐ at New York Jets 8:15 pm ___
Final Score: _____ v. _____

Teams with bye: Carolina Panthers, Cleveland Browns, Pittsburgh Steelers, Tampa Bay Buccaneers

k your winners before the games start, then keep track of the scores as they happen.

			✓ Your Correct Picks

ursday Night Game

☐ Washington Redskins	☐ at Minnesota Vikings	8:20 pm	___
Final Score: ___ v. ___			

nday Games

☐ Arizona Cardinals	☐ at New Orleans Saints	1 pm	___
Final Score: ___ v. ___			

☐ Cincinnati Bengals	☐ at Los Angeles Rams		___
Final Score: ___ v. ___			

☐ Los Angeles Chargers	☐ at Chicago Bears		___
Final Score: ___ v. ___			

☐ New York Giants	☐ at Detroit Lions		___
Final Score: ___ v. ___			

☐ New York Jets	☐ at Jacksonville Jaguars		___
Final Score: ___ v. ___			

☐ Oakland Raiders	☐ at Houston Texans		___
Final Score: ___ v. ___			

☐ Philadelphia Eagles	☐ at Buffalo Bills		___
Final Score: ___ v. ___			

☐ Seattle Seahawks	☐ at Atlanta Falcons		___
Final Score: ___ v. ___			

☐ Tampa Bay Buccaneers	☐ at Tennessee Titans		___
Final Score: ___ v. ___			

☐ Carolina Panthers	☐ at San Francisco 49ers	4 pm	___
Final Score: ___ v. ___			

☐ Cleveland Browns	☐ at New England Patriots		___
Final Score: ___ v. ___			

☐ Denver Broncos	☐ at Indianapolis Colts		___
Final Score: ___ v. ___			

nday Night Game

☐ Green Bay Packers	☐ at Kansas City Chiefs	8:20 pm	___
Final Score: ___ v. ___			

onday Night Game

☐ Miami Dolphins	☐ at Pittsburgh Steelers	8:15 pm	___
Final Score: ___ v. ___			

ams with bye: Baltimore Ravens, Dallas Cowboys

WEEK 9: October 31–November 4

Pick your winners before the games start, then keep track of the scores as they happ

Thursday Night Game			✓ Your Correct Pic
☐ San Francisco 49ers	☐ at Arizona Cardinals	8:20 pm	___
Final Score: _____ v. _____			

Sunday Games

☐ Houston Texans	☐ at Jacksonville Jaguars	9:30 am	___
Final Score: _____ v. _____			
☐ Chicago Bears	☐ at Philadelphia Eagles	1 pm	___
Final Score: _____ v. _____			
☐ Indianapolis Colts	☐ at Pittsburgh Steelers		___
Final Score: _____ v. _____			
☐ Minnesota Vikings	☐ at Kansas City Chiefs		___
Final Score: _____ v. _____			
☐ New York Jets	☐ at Miami Dolphins		___
Final Score: _____ v. _____			
☐ Tennessee Titans	☐ at Carolina Panthers		___
Final Score: _____ v. _____			
☐ Washington Redskins	☐ at Buffalo Bills		___
Final Score: _____ v. _____			
☐ Cleveland Browns	☐ at Denver Broncos	4 pm	___
Final Score: _____ v. _____			
☐ Detroit Lions	☐ at Oakland Raiders		___
Final Score: _____ v. _____			
☐ Green Bay Packers	☐ at Los Angeles Chargers		___
Final Score: _____ v. _____			
☐ Tampa Bay Buccaneers	☐ at Seattle Seahawks		___
Final Score: _____ v. _____			

Sunday Night Game

☐ New England Patriots	☐ at Baltimore Ravens	8:20 pm	___
Final Score: _____ v. _____			

Monday Night Game

☐ Dallas Cowboys	☐ at New York Giants	8:15 pm	___
Final Score: _____ v. _____			

Teams with bye: Atlanta Falcons, Cincinnati Bengals, Los Angeles Rams, New Orleans Saints

WEEK 10: November 7-11

k your winners before the games start, then keep track of the scores as they happen.

ırsday Night Game

☐ Los Angeles Chargers ☐ at Oakland Raiders 8:20 pm ___
    Final Score: _____ v. _____

ıday Games

☐ Arizona Cardinals ☐ at Tampa Bay Buccaneers 1 pm ___
    Final Score: _____ v. _____

☐ Atlanta Falcons ☐ at New Orleans Saints ___
    Final Score: _____ v. _____

☐ Baltimore Ravens ☐ at Cincinnati Bengals ___
    Final Score: _____ v. _____

☐ Buffalo Bills ☐ at Cleveland Browns ___
    Final Score: _____ v. _____

☐ Carolina Panthers ☐ at Green Bay Packers ___
    Final Score: _____ v. _____

☐ Detroit Lions ☐ at Chicago Bears ___
    Final Score: _____ v. _____

☐ Kansas City Chiefs ☐ at Tennessee Titans ___
    Final Score: _____ v. _____

☐ New York Giants ☐ at New York Jets ___
    Final Score: _____ v. _____

☐ Los Angeles Rams ☐ at Pittsburgh Steelers 4 pm ___
    Final Score: _____ v. _____

☐ Miami Dolphins ☐ at Indianapolis Colts ___
    Final Score: _____ v. _____

ıday Night Game

☐ Minnesota Vikings ☐ at Dallas Cowboys 8:20 pm ___
    Final Score: _____ v. _____

ınday Night Game

☐ Seattle Seahawks ☐ at San Francisco 49ers 8:15 pm ___
    Final Score: _____ v. _____

ams with bye: Denver Broncos, Houston Texans, Jacksonville Jaguars, New England Patriots, Philadelphia Eagles, Washington Redskins

WEEK 11: November 14-18

Pick your winners before the games start, then keep track of the scores as they happ

Thursday Night Game

☐ Pittsburgh Steelers ☐ at Cleveland Browns 8:20 pm ____
Final Score: _____ v. _____

Sunday Games

☐ Atlanta Falcons ☐ at Carolina Panthers 1 pm ____
Final Score: _____ v. _____

☐ Buffalo Bills ☐ at Miami Dolphins ____
Final Score: _____ v. _____

☐ Dallas Cowboys ☐ at Detroit Lions ____
Final Score: _____ v. _____

☐ Denver Broncos ☐ at Minnesota Vikings ____
Final Score: _____ v. _____

☐ Houston Texans ☐ at Baltimore Ravens ____
Final Score: _____ v. _____

☐ Jacksonville Jaguars ☐ at Indianapolis Colts ____
Final Score: _____ v. _____

☐ New Orleans Saints ☐ at Tampa Bay Buccaneers ____
Final Score: _____ v. _____

☐ New York Jets ☐ at Washington Redskins ____
Final Score: _____ v. _____

☐ Arizona Cardinals ☐ at San Francisco 49ers 4 pm ____
Final Score: _____ v. _____

☐ Cincinnati Bengals ☐ at Oakland Raiders ____
Final Score: _____ v. _____

☐ New England Patriots ☐ at Philadelphia Eagles ____
Final Score: _____ v. _____

Sunday Night Game

☐ Chicago Bears ☐ at Los Angeles Rams 8:20 pm ____
Final Score: _____ v. _____

Monday Night Game

☐ Kansas City Chiefs ☐ at Los Angeles Chargers 8:15 pm ____
Final Score: _____ v. _____

Teams with bye: Green Bay Packers, New York Giants, Seattle Seahawks,
Tennessee Titans

WEEK 12: November 21-25

k your winners before the games start, then keep track of the scores as they happen.

			✓ Your Correct Picks

ursday Night Game

☐ Indianapolis Colts   ☐ at Houston Texans   8:20 pm   ____
Final Score: _____ v. _____

nday Games

☐ Carolina Panthers   ☐ at New Orleans Saints   1 pm   ____
Final Score: _____ v. _____

☐ Denver Broncos   ☐ at Buffalo Bills   ____
Final Score: _____ v. _____

☐ Detroit Lions   ☐ at Washington Redskins   ____
Final Score: _____ v. _____

☐ Miami Dolphins   ☐ at Cleveland Browns   ____
Final Score: _____ v. _____

☐ New York Giants   ☐ at Chicago Bears   ____
Final Score: _____ v. _____

☐ Oakland Raiders   ☐ at New York Jets   ____
Final Score: _____ v. _____

☐ Pittsburgh Steelers   ☐ at Cincinnati Bengals   - ____
Final Score: _____ v. _____

☐ Tampa Bay Buccaneers   ☐ at Atlanta Falcons   ____
Final Score: _____ v. _____

☐ Dallas Cowboys   ☐ at New England Patriots   4 pm   ____
Final Score: _____ v. _____

☐ Green Bay Packers   ☐ at San Francisco 49ers   ____
Final Score: _____ v. _____

☐ Jacksonville Jaguars   ☐ at Tennessee Titans   ____
Final Score: _____ v. _____

nday Night Game

☐ Seattle Seahawks   ☐ at Philadelphia Eagles   8:20 pm   ____
Final Score: _____ v. _____

onday Night Game

☐ Baltimore Ravens   ☐ at Los Angeles Rams   8:15 pm   ____
Final Score: _____ v. _____

ams with bye: Arizona Cardinals, Kansas City Chiefs, Los Angeles Chargers, Minnesota Vikings

WEEK 13: November 28-December 2

Pick your winners before the games start, then keep track of the scores as they happ

Thanksgiving Day Games

☐ Chicago Bears ☐ at Detroit Lions 12:30 pm ___
Final Score: _____ v. _____

☐ Buffalo Bills ☐ at Dallas Cowboys 4:30 pm ___
Final Score: _____ v. _____

☐ New Orleans Saints ☐ at Atlanta Falcons 8:20 pm ___
Final Score: _____ v. _____

Sunday Games

☐ Green Bay Packers ☐ at New York Giants 1 pm ___
Final Score: _____ v. _____

☐ New York Jets ☐ at Cincinnati Bengals ___
Final Score: _____ v. _____

☐ Oakland Raiders ☐ at Kansas City Chiefs ___
Final Score: _____ v. _____

☐ Philadelphia Eagles ☐ at Miami Dolphins ___
Final Score: _____ v. _____

☐ San Francisco 49ers ☐ at Baltimore Ravens ___
Final Score: _____ v. _____

☐ Tampa Bay Buccaneers ☐ at Jacksonville Jaguars ___
Final Score: _____ v. _____

☐ Tennessee Titans ☐ at Indianapolis Colts ___
Final Score: _____ v. _____

☐ Washington Redskins ☐ at Carolina Panthers ___
Final Score: _____ v. _____

☐ Cleveland Browns ☐ at Pittsburgh Steelers 4 pm ___
Final Score: _____ v. _____

☐ Los Angeles Chargers ☐ at Denver Broncos ___
Final Score: _____ v. _____

☐ Los Angeles Rams ☐ at Arizona Cardinals ___
Final Score: _____ v. _____

Sunday Night Game

☐ New England Patriots ☐ at Houston Texans 8:20 pm ___
Final Score: _____ v. _____

Monday Night Game

☐ Minnesota Vikings ☐ at Seattle Seahawks 8:15 pm ___
Final Score: _____ v. _____

WEEK 14: December 5-9

k your winners before the games start, then keep track of the scores as they happen.

			✓ Your Correct Picks

ursday Night Game

☐ Dallas Cowboys ☐ at Chicago Bears 8:20 pm ___
Final Score: ___ v. ___

nday Games

☐ Baltimore Ravens ☐ at Buffalo Bills 1 pm ___
Final Score: ___ v. ___

☐ Carolina Panthers ☐ at Atlanta Falcons ___
Final Score: ___ v. ___

☐ Cincinnati Bengals ☐ at Cleveland Browns ___
Final Score: ___ v. ___

☐ Denver Broncos ☐ at Houston Texans ___
Final Score: ___ v. ___

☐ Detroit Lions ☐ at Minnesota Vikings ___
Final Score: ___ v. ___

☐ Indianapolis Colts ☐ at Tampa Bay Buccaneers ___
Final Score: ___ v. ___

☐ Miami Dolphins ☐ at New York Jets ___
Final Score: ___ v. ___

☐ San Francisco 49ers ☐ at New Orleans Saints ___
Final Score: ___ v. ___

☐ Washington Redskins ☐ at Green Bay Packers ___
Final Score: ___ v. ___

☐ Kansas City Chiefs ☐ at New England Patriots 4 pm ___
Final Score: ___ v. ___

☐ Los Angeles Chargers ☐ at Jacksonville Jaguars ___
Final Score: ___ v. ___

☐ Pittsburgh Steelers ☐ at Arizona Cardinals ___
Final Score: ___ v. ___

☐ Tennessee Titans ☐ at Oakland Raiders ___
Final Score: ___ v. ___

nday Night Game

☐ Seattle Seahawks ☐ at Los Angeles Rams 8:20 pm ___
Final Score: ___ v. ___

»nday Night Game

☐ New York Giants ☐ at Philadelphia Eagles 8:15 pm ___
Final Score: ___ v. ___

WEEK 15: December 12-16

Pick your winners before the games start, then keep track of the scores as they happ

Thursday Night Game

☐ New York Jets ☐ at Baltimore Ravens 8:20 pm ___
Final Score: _____ v. _____

Sunday Games

☐ Buffalo Bills ☐ at Pittsburgh Steelers 1 pm ___
Final Score: _____ v. _____

☐ Chicago Bears ☐ at Green Bay Packers ___
Final Score: _____ v. _____

☐ Denver Broncos ☐ at Kansas City Chiefs ___
Final Score: _____ v. _____

☐ Houston Texans ☐ at Tennessee Titans ___
Final Score: _____ v. _____

☐ Miami Dolphins ☐ at New York Giants ___
Final Score: _____ v. _____

☐ New England Patriots ☐ at Cincinnati Bengals ___
Final Score: _____ v. _____

☐ Philadelphia Eagles ☐ at Washington Redskins ___
Final Score: _____ v. _____

☐ Seattle Seahawks ☐ at Carolina Panthers ___
Final Score: _____ v. _____

☐ Tampa Bay Buccaneers ☐ at Detroit Lions ___
Final Score: _____ v. _____

☐ Atlanta Falcons ☐ at San Francisco 49ers 4 pm ___
Final Score: _____ v. _____

☐ Cleveland Browns ☐ at Arizona Cardinals ___
Final Score: _____ v. _____

☐ Jacksonville Jaguars ☐ at Oakland Raiders ___
Final Score: _____ v. _____

☐ Los Angeles Rams ☐ at Dallas Cowboys ___
Final Score: _____ v. _____

Sunday Night Game

☐ Minnesota Vikings ☐ at Los Angeles Chargers 8:20 pm ___
Final Score: _____ v. _____

Monday Night Game

☐ Indianapolis Colts ☐ at New Orleans Saints 8:15 pm ___
Final Score: _____ v. _____

WEEK 16: December 22-23

k your winners before the games start, then keep track of the scores as they happen.

			✓ Your Correct Picks

nday Games

☐ Baltimore Ravens ☐ at Cleveland Browns 1 pm ___
    Final Score: _____ v. _____

☐ Buffalo Bills ☐ at New England Patriots ___
    Final Score: _____ v. _____

☐ Carolina Panthers ☐ at Indianapolis Colts ___
    Final Score: _____ v. _____

☐ Cincinnati Bengals ☐ at Miami Dolphins ___
    Final Score: _____ v. _____

☐ Detroit Lions ☐ at Denver Broncos ___
    Final Score: _____ v. _____

☐ Houston Texans ☐ at Tampa Bay Buccaneers ___
    Final Score: _____ v. _____

☐ Jacksonville Jaguars ☐ at Atlanta Falcons ___
    Final Score: _____ v. _____

☐ Los Angeles Rams ☐ at San Francisco 49ers ___
    Final Score: _____ v. _____

☐ New Orleans Saints ☐ at Tennessee Titans ___
    Final Score: _____ v. _____

☐ New York Giants ☐ at Washington Redskins ___
    Final Score: _____ v. _____

☐ Oakland Raiders ☐ at Los Angeles Chargers ___
    Final Score: _____ v. _____

☐ Pittsburgh Steelers ☐ at New York Jets ___
    Final Score: _____ v. _____

☐ Arizona Cardinals ☐ at Seattle Seahawks 4 pm ___
    Final Score: _____ v. _____

☐ Dallas Cowboys ☐ at Philadelphia Eagles ___
    Final Score: _____ v. _____

nday Night Game

☐ Kansas City Chiefs ☐ at Chicago Bears 8:20 pm ___
    Final Score: _____ v. _____

nday Night Game

☐ Green Bay Packers ☐ at Minnesota Vikings 8:15 pm ___
    Final Score: _____ v. _____

23

WEEK 17: December 29

Pick your winners before the games start, then keep track of the scores as they happ

Sunday Games

☐ Atlanta Falcons ☐ at Tampa Bay Buccaneers 1 pm ____
Final Score: _____ v. _____

☐ Chicago Bears ☐ at Minnesota Vikings ____
Final Score: _____ v. _____

☐ Cleveland Browns ☐ at Cincinnati Bengals ____
Final Score: _____ v. _____

☐ Green Bay Packers ☐ at Detroit Lions ____
Final Score: _____ v. _____

☐ Indianapolis Colts ☐ at Jacksonville Jaguars ____
Final Score: _____ v. _____

☐ Los Angeles Chargers ☐ at Kansas City Chiefs ____
Final Score: _____ v. _____

☐ Miami Dolphins ☐ at New England Patriots ____
Final Score: _____ v. _____

☐ New Orleans Saints ☐ at Carolina Panthers ____
Final Score: _____ v. _____

☐ New York Jets ☐ at Buffalo Bills ____
Final Score: _____ v. _____

☐ Philadelphia Eagles ☐ at New York Giants ____
Final Score: _____ v. _____

☐ Pittsburgh Steelers ☐ at Baltimore Ravens ____
Final Score: _____ v. _____

☐ Tennessee Titans ☐ at Houston Texans ____
Final Score: _____ v. _____

☐ Washington Redskins ☐ at Dallas Cowboys ____
Final Score: _____ v. _____

☐ Arizona Cardinals ☐ at Los Angeles Rams 4:25 pm ____
Final Score: _____ v. _____

☐ Oakland Raiders ☐ at Denver Broncos ____
Final Score: _____ v. _____

☐ San Francisco 49ers ☐ at Seattle Seahawks ____
Final Score: _____ v. _____

TEAM SCHEDULES

25

*new co‹

Arizona showed no patience for their first-year head coach *or* their new rookie quarterback; after a season that landed the Cardinals in last place in the NFL, the Bidwills sent both Steve Wilks and Josh Rosen packing. But are we sure this new plan is going to work? Yes, Kyler Murray has exceptional skills, but can a 5'9" quarterback make it in the NFL? For that matter, what exactly is Kliff Kingsbury *doing* in the NFL? After getting fired by Texas Tech, he signed on with USC as offensive coordinator, only to leave them after six weeks for his first gig as *any* kind of coach in the National Football League, never mind head coach. Yes, he coached up Baker Mayfield, Davis Webb and Patty Mahomes in college (OK, that is pretty remarkable), but he will have to do much more than be a quarterback whisperer as head coach of the Cardinals. Meanwhile, Larry Fitzgerald graciously puts up with yet another regime change, and yet another season that promises to be more of a rebuild than a run for the gold.

ARIZONA CARDINALS

TEAM SCHEDULE
Arizona Cardinals

ep track of wins and losses **(division games in bold)**

				W/L	RUNNING TOTAL
eek 1	Sun, Sep 8	4:25 PM	Detroit Lions	___	___/___
eek 2	Sun, Sep 15	1:00 PM	at Baltimore Ravens	___	___/___
eek 3	Sun, Sep 22	4:05 PM	Carolina Panthers	___	___/___
eek 4	**Sun, Sep 29**	**4:05 PM**	**Seattle Seahawks**	___	___/___
eek 5	Sun, Oct 6	1:00 PM	at Cincinnati Bengals	___	___/___
eek 6	Sun, Oct 13	4:05 PM	Atlanta Falcons	___	___/___
eek 7	Sun, Oct 20	1:00 PM	at New York Giants	___	___/___
eek 8	Sun, Oct 27	1:00 PM	at New Orleans Saints	___	___/___
eek 9	**Thu, Oct 31**	**8:20 PM**	**San Francisco 49ers**	___	___/___
eek 10	Sun, Nov 10	1:00 PM	at Tampa Bay Buccaneers	___	___/___
eek 11	**Sun, Nov 17**	**4:05 PM**	**at San Francisco 49ers**	___	___/___
eek 12	BYE WEEK				
eek 13	**Sun, Dec 1**	**4:05 PM**	**Los Angeles Rams**	___	___/___
eek 14	Sun, Dec 8	4:25 PM	Pittsburgh Steelers	___	___/___
eek 15	Sun, Dec 15	4:05 PM	Cleveland Browns	___	___/___
eek 16	**Sun, Dec 22**	**4:25 PM**	**at Seattle Seahawks**	___	___/___
eek 17	**Sun, Dec 29**	**4:25 PM**	**at Los Angeles Rams**	___	___/___

END OF SEASON RECORD:___/___

DIVISION TOTAL WIN/LOSS: ___/___

ATLANTA FALCONS

Head Coach: Dan Quinn | 2018 Record: 7-9
First Round Draft Picks: Chris Lindstrom – G (14); Kaleb McGary – T (3

The injury bug bit hard in Atlanta last year, with Devonta Freeman, Keanu Neal, Ricardo Allen, Deion Jones, and Andy Levitre all suffering injuries that kept the Falcons from ever getting any momentum. Julio Jones surprised exactly no one by excelling once again — ranking #1 among all wide receivers in passing yards (1,677) and becoming the only receiver in the league to average more than 100 receiving yards per game, in this, his 8th season. (And happily, it looks like he will get paid for being the best, as the Falcons near a long-term contract extension with Jones.) Quarterback Matt Ryan played well, racking up 4,924 yards (making him the third best passer, behind only Patrick Mahomes and Ben Roethlisberger), but the team as a whole couldn't seem to gel when they needed to. As they enter 2019, Atlanta still looks strong on paper — their two first-round picks should significantly help the offensive line, while last year's first round pick, WR Calvin Ridley showed flashes of brilliance last year, despite dropping too many balls he should have caught. If they can clean things up, the Falcons should contend for a playoff spot in 2019.

ATLANTA FALCONS

TEAM SCHEDULE
Atlanta Falcons

				W/L	RUNNING TOTAL
ep track of wins and losses *(division games in bold)*					
eek 1	Sun, Sep 8	1:00 PM	at Minnesota Vikings	___	___/___
eek 2	Sun, Sep 15	8:20 PM	Philadelphia Eagles	___	___/___
eek 3	Sun, Sep 22	1:00 PM	at Indianapolis Colts	___	___/___
eek 4	Sun, Sep 29	1:00 PM	Tennessee Titans	___	___/___
eek 5	Sun, Oct 6	1:00 PM	at Houston Texans	___	___/___
eek 6	Sun, Oct 13	4:05 PM	at Arizona Cardinals	___	___/___
eek 7	Sun, Oct 20	1:00 PM	Los Angeles Rams	___	___/___
eek 8	Sun, Oct 27	1:00 PM	Seattle Seahawks	___	___/___
eek 9	BYE WEEK				
eek 10	**Sun, Nov 10**	**1:00 PM**	**at New Orleans Saints**	___	___/___
eek 11	**Sun, Nov 17**	**1:00 PM**	**at Carolina Panthers**	___	___/___
eek 12	**Sun, Nov 24**	**1:00 PM**	**Tampa Bay Buccaneers**	___	___/___
eek 13	**Thu, Nov 28**	**8:20 PM**	**New Orleans Saints**	___	___/___
eek 14	**Sun, Dec 8**	**1:00 PM**	**Carolina Panthers**	___	___/___
eek 15	Sun, Dec 15	4:25 PM	at San Francisco 49ers	___	___/___
eek 16	Sun, Dec 22	1:00 PM	Jacksonville Jaguars	___	___/___
eek 17	**Sun, Dec 29**	**1:00 PM**	**at Tampa Bay Buccaneers**	___	___/___

END OF SEASON RECORD:___/___

DIVISION TOTAL WIN/LOSS: ___/___

BALTIMORE RAVENS

Head Coach: John Harbaugh | 2018 Record: 10-6
First Round Draft Pick: Marquise Brown - WR (25)

Bye-bye Joe Flacco, thanks for all you've done, but we are *turning the page*. John Harbaugh has thrown his chips down on QB Lamar Jackson, and the Ravens have now committed to a very different style of play offensively than during the Flacco era. But even though Jackson took over the reins in week 11 of last season, it's not clear the Ravens have figured out how to make this scramble-first, run-heavy, tricky-dicky offense sustainable. Winning the AFC North last year had as much to do with Pittsburgh choking as Baltimore excelling, and it's Baltimore's defense that proved stout when it counted — coming in as the best defense in the league for total yards allowed per game. As we look ahead to 2019, Harbaugh is clearly hoping that newly-signed powerback Mark Ingram will take some pressure off Jackson. That's certainly a good start. And we love the talent and flash of Marquise "Hollywood" Brown — but can Baltimore make the most of him with a quarterback who'd rather run than throw? Let's just say we are not convinced the Ravens offense has a recipe for success.

BALTIMORE RAVENS

TEAM SCHEDULE
Baltimore Ravens

ep track of wins and losses **(division games in bold)**

				W/L	RUNNING TOTAL
eek 1	Sun, Sep 8	1:00 PM	at Miami Dolphins	___	___/___
eek 2	Sun, Sep 15	1:00 PM	Arizona Cardinals	___	___/___
eek 3	Sun, Sep 22	1:00 PM	at Kansas City Chiefs	___	___/___
eek 4	**Sun, Sep 29**	**1:00 PM**	**Cleveland Browns**	___	___/___
eek 5	**Sun, Oct 6**	**1:00 PM**	**at Pittsburgh Steelers**	___	___/___
eek 6	**Sun, Oct 13**	**1:00 PM**	**Cincinnati Bengals**	___	___/___
eek 7	Sun, Oct 20	4:25 PM	at Seattle Seahawks	___	___/___
eek 8	BYE WEEK				
eek 9	Sun, Nov 3	8:20 PM	New England Patriots	___	___/___
eek 10	**Sun, Nov 10**	**1:00 PM**	**at Cincinnati Bengals**	___	___/___
eek 11	Sun, Nov 17	1:00 PM	Houston Texans	___	___/___
eek 12	Mon, Nov 25	8:15 PM	at Los Angeles Rams	___	___/___
eek 13	Sun, Dec 1	1:00 PM	San Francisco 49ers	___	___/___
eek 14	Sun, Dec 8	1:00 PM	at Buffalo Bills	___	___/___
eek 15	Thu, Dec 12	8:20 PM	New York Jets	___	___/___
eek 16	**Sun, Dec 22**	**1:00 PM**	**at Cleveland Browns**	___	___/___
eek 17	**Sun, Dec 29**	**1:00 PM**	**Pittsburgh Steelers**	___	___/___

END OF SEASON RECORD:___/___

DIVISION TOTAL WIN/LOSS: ___/___

BUFFALO BILLS

Head Coach: Sean McDermott | 2018 Record: 6-10
First Round Draft Pick: Ed Oliver – DT (9)

2018 was a challenging year for the Bills, a step backwards in terms of their record, and a clear step into a new era with QB Josh Allen. The jury is most definitely still out on whether he will prove to be the franchise quarterback Buffalo hoped when they drafted him at #7 in 2018, and the offense as a whole was pretty miserable, ranking in the bottom five for points per game, yards per game, and touchdowns (where they were dead last at only 13 TD's all season). But Buffalo's defense was surprisingly strong, allowing the second fewest total yards per game among all teams in the NFL, and that defense should only get better with first-round pick Ed Oliver at defensive tackle. Still, Buffalo needs some juice on offense. They hope to get help from Cole Beasley, John Brown, T.J. Yeldon and Frank Gore — as well as rookies Devin Singletary and Dawson Knox. That's a lot of pieces, but we're not counting on the Bills to contend for their division anytime soon.

BUFFALO BILLS

TEAM SCHEDULE
Buffalo Bills

				RUNNING
ep track of wins and losses *(division games in bold)*			W/L	TOTAL
eek 1	**Sun, Sep 8**	**1:00 PM**	**at New York Jets**	___ ___/___
eek 2	Sun, Sep 15	1:00 PM	at New York Giants	___ ___/___
eek 3	Sun, Sep 22	1:00 PM	Cincinnati Bengals	___ ___/___
eek 4	**Sun, Sep 29**	**1:00 PM**	**New England Patriots**	___ ___/___
eek 5	Sun, Oct 6	1:00 PM	at Tennessee Titans	___ ___/___
eek 6	BYE WEEK			
eek 7	**Sun, Oct 20**	**1:00 PM**	**Miami Dolphins**	___ ___/___
eek 8	Sun, Oct 27	1:00 PM	Philadelphia Eagles	___ ___/___
eek 9	Sun, Nov 3	1:00 PM	Washington Redskins	___ ___/___
eek 10	Sun, Nov 10	1:00 PM	at Cleveland Browns	___ ___/___
eek 11	**Sun, Nov 17**	**1:00 PM**	**at Miami Dolphins**	___ ___/___
eek 12	Sun, Nov 24	1:00 PM	Denver Broncos	___ ___/___
eek 13	Thu, Nov 28	4:30 PM	at Dallas Cowboys	___ ___/___
eek 14	Sun, Dec 8	1:00 PM	Baltimore Ravens	___ ___/___
eek 15	Sun, Dec 15	1:00 PM	at Pittsburgh Steelers	___ ___/___
eek 16	**Sun, Dec 22**	**1:00 PM**	**at New England Patriots**	___ ___/___
eek 17	**Sun, Dec 29**	**1:00 PM**	**New York Jets**	___ ___/___

END OF SEASON RECORD:___/___

DIVISION TOTAL WIN/LOSS: ___/___

CAROLINA PANTHERS

Head Coach: Ron Rivera | 2018 Record: 7-9
First Round Draft Pick: Brian Burns – DE (16)

Cam Newton was playing hurt! That's why he was so puzzlingly inconsistent and interception-prone last year. Now he's had that shoulder surgery, and early reports say he looks great. That's exactly what the Panthers will need in order to get back to the playoffs in 2019. Their young running back Christian McCaffrey is for real, their young receiver D.J. More is excellent — and of course their star defensive player, Luke Kuechly, provides both excellence and inspiration, as long as he can avoid those concussions that have plagued him. In sum, if Cam is sharp, Carolina should bounce back in 2019. Unfortunately for them, they have both Atlanta and New Orleans to deal with.

CAROLINA PANTHERS

Carolina Panthers

				W/L	RUNNING TOTAL
ep track of wins and losses *(division games in bold)*					
ek 1	Sun, Sep 8	1:00 PM	Los Angeles Rams	___	___/___
ek 2	**Thu, Sep 12**	**8:20 PM**	**Tampa Bay Buccaneers**	___	___/___
ek 3	Sun, Sep 22	4:05 PM	at Arizona Cardinals	___	___/___
ek 4	Sun, Sep 29	1:00 PM	at Houston Texans	___	___/___
ek 5	Sun, Oct 6	1:00 PM	Jacksonville Jaguars	___	___/___
ek 6	**Sun, Oct 13**	**9:30 AM**	**at Tampa Bay Buccaneers**	___	___/___
ek 7	BYE WEEK				
ek 8	Sun, Oct 27	4:05 PM	at San Francisco 49ers	___	___/___
ek 9	Sun, Nov 3	1:00 PM	Tennessee Titans	___	___/___
ek 10	Sun, Nov 10	1:00 PM	at Green Bay Packers	___	___/___
eek 11	**Sun, Nov 17**	**1:00 PM**	**Atlanta Falcons**	___	___/___
eek 12	**Sun, Nov 24**	**1:00 PM**	**at New Orleans Saints**	___	___/___
eek 13	Sun, Dec 1	1:00 PM	Washington Redskins	___	___/___
eek 14	**Sun, Dec 8**	**1:00 PM**	**at Atlanta Falcons**	___	___/___
eek 15	Sun, Dec 15	1:00 PM	Seattle Seahawks	___	___/___
eek 16	Sun, Dec 22	1:00 PM	at Indianapolis Colts	___	___/___
eek 17	**Sun, Dec 29**	**1:00 PM**	**New Orleans Saints**	___	___/___

END OF SEASON RECORD:___/___

DIVISION TOTAL WIN/LOSS: ___/___

CHICAGO BEARS

Head Coach: Matt Nagy | 2018 Record: 12-4

First Round Draft Pick: No Picks in Round 1

If we'd had a vote, we would have chosen Matt Nagy, too. As head coach of the year *in his first year*, Nagy inspired his club to a terrific 12-4 record, going from worst to first in a division that has some very serious competition. The Bears started out the season with a blockbuster trade — signing Khalil Mack to a giant $141-million six-year deal. Needless to say, quarterbacks were a whole lot less excited about their visits to Soldier Field. If they could get the ball out before an unpleasant meeting with Khalil Mack, they had to face two of the top five players in the league at intercepting the ball: Kyle Fuller and Eddie Jackson. Overall, Chicago's defense was among the best — in fact, they were *the* best at rushing defense and interceptions. Chicago comes into 2019 looking strong, and even though QB Mitch Trubisky didn't have a stellar year-two, he proved the stage is not too big, and we believe he will continue to improve.

CHICAGO BEARS

Chicago Bears

				W/L	RUNNING TOTAL
ep track of wins and losses *(division games in bold)*					
eek 1	**Thu, Sep 5**	**8:20 PM**	**Green Bay Packers**	___	___/___
eek 2	Sun, Sep 15	4:25 PM	at Denver Broncos	___	___/___
eek 3	Mon, Sep 23	8:15 PM	at Washington Redskins	___	___/___
eek 4	**Sun, Sep 29**	**4:25 PM**	**Minnesota Vikings**	___	___/___
eek 5	Sun, Oct 6	1:00 PM	at Oakland Raiders	___	___/___
eek 6	BYE WEEK				
eek 7	Sun, Oct 20	4:25 PM	New Orleans Saints	___	___/___
eek 8	Sun, Oct 27	1:00 PM	Los Angeles Chargers	___	___/___
eek 9	Sun, Nov 3	1:00 PM	at Philadelphia Eagles	___	___/___
eek 10	**Sun, Nov 10**	**1:00 PM**	**Detroit Lions**	___	___/___
eek 11	Sun, Nov 17	8:20 PM	at Los Angeles Rams	___	___/___
eek 12	Sun, Nov 24	1:00 PM	New York Giants	___	___/___
eek 13	**Thu, Nov 28**	**12:30 PM**	**at Detroit Lions**	___	___/___
eek 14	Thu, Dec 5	8:20 PM	Dallas Cowboys	___	___/___
eek 15	**Sun, Dec 15**	**1:00 PM**	**at Green Bay Packers**	___	___/___
eek 16	Sun, Dec 22	8:20 PM	Kansas City Chiefs	___	___/___
eek 17	**Sun, Dec 29**	**1:00 PM**	**at Minnesota Vikings**	___	___/___

END OF SEASON RECORD:___/___

DIVISION TOTAL WIN/LOSS: ___/___

CINCINNATI BENGALS

Head Coach: Zac Taylor* | 2018 Record: 6-10
First Round Draft Pick: Jonah Williams – T (11)

*new co

At last. Fans of this guide know we've been calling for this for years, but *at last* the Bengals threw in the towel on head coach Marv Lewis. So now what? New HC Zac Taylor is one of the new breed of young, offensive-minded head coaches that everyone is in love with, but does he have the management experience to make this work? He was quarterbacks coach for the Rams last year, for just one year, and his resume beyond that is...thin. Taylor takes over a team with questions at quarterback (is Andy Dalton the guy?) and a defense that was pretty dismal in 2019 (bottom five against the run, and dead last in total yards allowed per game). There are some promising notes — Dalton was actually having one of his best years before his season-ending injury, and RB Joe Mixon came on really strong, but we believe the Bengals still have a long road to get back to the playoffs. Meanwhile, bad news struck early for the Bengals: Jonah Williams, their promising first-round pick, slotted to start at the all-important left tackle position, had surgery before training camp even began and will be out for the season. It happens to teams every year, and now the Bengals' road looks even longer than before.

CINCINNATI BENGALS

TEAM SCHEDULE
Cincinnati Bengals

ep track of wins and losses (division games in bold)				W/L	RUNNING TOTAL
eek 1	Sun, Sep 8	4:05 PM	at Seattle Seahawks	___	___/___
eek 2	Sun, Sep 15	1:00 PM	San Francisco 49ers	___	___/___
eek 3	Sun, Sep 22	1:00 PM	at Buffalo Bills	___	___/___
eek 4	**Mon, Sep 30**	**8:15 PM**	**at Pittsburgh Steelers**	___	___/___
eek 5	Sun, Oct 6	1:00 PM	Arizona Cardinals	___	___/___
eek 6	**Sun, Oct 13**	**1:00 PM**	**at Baltimore Ravens**	___	___/___
eek 7	Sun, Oct 20	1:00 PM	Jacksonville Jaguars	___	___/___
eek 8	Sun, Oct 27	1:00 PM	at Los Angeles Rams	___	___/___
eek 9	BYE WEEK				
eek 10	**Sun, Nov 10**	**1:00 PM**	**Baltimore Ravens**	___	___/___
eek 11	Sun, Nov 17	4:25 PM	at Oakland Raiders	___	___/___
eek 12	**Sun, Nov 24**	**1:00 PM**	**Pittsburgh Steelers**	___	___/___
eek 13	Sun, Dec 1	1:00 PM	New York Jets	___	___/___
eek 14	**Sun, Dec 8**	**1:00 PM**	**at Cleveland Browns**	___	___/___
eek 15	Sun, Dec 15	1:00 PM	New England Patriots	___	___/___
eek 16	Sun, Dec 22	1:00 PM	at Miami Dolphins	___	___/___
eek 17	**Sun, Dec 29**	**1:00 PM**	**Cleveland Browns**	___	___/___

END OF SEASON RECORD:___/___

DIVISION TOTAL WIN/LOSS: ___/___

CLEVELAND BROWNS
Head Coach: Freddie Kitchens* | 2018 Record: 7-8-
First Round Draft Pick: No Picks in Round 1

*new co

There is new life in Cleveland! In fact, there is a whole lot of excitement. Rookie QB Baker Mayfield lit. it. up. — proving the Browns actually *did* know what they were doing taking him #1 in the draft. And just in case you thought that was a fluke, their #4 pick in the draft, cornerback Denzel Ward, and their second-round pick, RB Nick Chubb, also proved to be terrific. Second-year defender Myles Garrett had 15 sacks, and altogether you have the makings of a very good, very young, very athletic defense in Cleveland. (No surprise they ranked at the top of the league in fumbles recovered in 2018.) And just in case Chubb wasn't enough, the Browns signed star rusher Kareem Hunt in the off-season, who will provide a fresh burst of offense when he's eligible to return to play for the second half of the season. But the really big news for 2019 was the signing of Odell Beckham Jr. Giving May-field a generational receiver could be the difference between a good year and a division-winning year. That's a lot to ask of first-year head coach Freddie Kitchens, but ever since he took over the offense (after Hu Jackson was fired) all arrows have been pointing to finally getting back to the playoffs. It's been a long time since Browns fans have had *that* on their horizon.

CLEVELAND BROWNS

TEAM SCHEDULE
Cleveland Browns

				W/L	RUNNING TOTAL
*ep track of wins and losses (**division games in bold**)*

				W/L	RUNNING TOTAL
₂ek 1	Sun, Sep 8	1:00 PM	Tennessee Titans	___	___/___
₂ek 2	Mon, Sep 16	8:15 PM	at New York Jets	___	___/___
₂ek 3	Sun, Sep 22	8:20 PM	Los Angeles Rams	___	___/___
₂ek 4	**Sun, Sep 29**	**1:00 PM**	**at Baltimore Ravens**	___	___/___
₂ek 5	Mon, Oct 7	8:15 PM	at San Francisco 49ers	___	___/___
₂ek 6	Sun, Oct 13	1:00 PM	Seattle Seahawks	___	___/___
₂ek 7	BYE WEEK				
₂ek 8	Sun, Oct 27	4:25 PM	at New England Patriots	___	___/___
₂ek 9	Sun, Nov. 3	4:25 PM	at Denver Broncos	___	___/___
₂ek 10	Sun, Nov 10	1:00 PM	Buffalo Bills	___	___/___
₂ek 11	**Thu, Nov 14**	**8:20 PM**	**Pittsburgh Steelers**	___	___/___
₂ek 12	Sun, Nov 24	1:00 PM	Miami Dolphins	___	___/___
₂ek 13	**Sun, Dec 1**	**4:25 PM**	**at Pittsburgh Steelers**	___	___/___
₂ek 14	**Sun, Dec 8**	**1:00 PM**	**Cincinnati Bengals**	___	___/___
₂ek 15	Sun, Dec 15	4:05 PM	at Arizona Cardinals	___	___/___
₂ek 16	**Sun, Dec 22**	**1:00 PM**	**Baltimore Ravens**	___	___/___
₂ek 17	**Sun, Dec 29**	**1:00 PM**	**at Cincinnati Bengals**	___	___/___

END OF SEASON RECORD:___/___

DIVISION TOTAL WIN/LOSS: ___/___

DALLAS COWBOYS

Head Coach: Jason Garrett | 2018 Record: 10-6
First Round Draft Pick: No Picks in Round 1

You gotta love Jerry Jones. When he's in, he's all in. And it looks like he's all in on QB Dak Prescott, who may soon join the ranks of the elite QBs in the NFL — at least in terms of how much he gets paid. Honestly, we like Dak, and we are rooting for him to have more tools around him this year to make the most of Dallas' excellent offensive line and excellent defense. Thanks to adding Amari Cooper last year, Dallas sat out the first round of the draft, but they did pick up Randall Cobb, the outstanding Green Bay WR and Tavon Austin, another talented receiver. And just when you thought he might be getting the hang of things on *Monday Night Football*, Jason Witten decided that life on the field was more attractive than on camera — so Dallas' best tight end will try to stage a come-back. Meanwhile, despite the criticism, Jerry has drafted really, really well — including the risk he took on Jaylon Smith a couple years ago. Smith, as well as last year's rookie Leighton Vander Esch (third best tackler *in the league* in 2018), made Dallas a top-five defense for rushing yards allowed in 2018. All in all, the Cowboys look stacked with talent. Now heads turn back to Dak, to see if he can truly step up and take the mantle of Pro Bowl caliber QB for America's team.

DALLAS COWBOYS

TEAM SCHEDULE
Dallas Cowboys

				W/L	RUNNING TOTAL
ep track of wins and losses *(division games in bold)*					
eek 1	**Sun, Sep 8**	**4:25 PM**	**New York Giants**	___	___/___
eek 2	**Sun, Sep 15**	**1:00 PM**	**at Washington Redskins**	___	___/___
eek 3	Sun, Sep 22	1:00 PM	Miami Dolphins	___	___/___
eek 4	Sun, Sep 29	8:20 PM	at New Orleans Saints	___	___/___
eek 5	Sun, Oct 6	4:25 PM	Green Bay Packers	___	___/___
eek 6	Sun, Oct 13	4:25 PM	at New York Jets	___	___/___
eek 7	**Sun, Oct 20**	**8:20 PM**	**Philadelphia Eagles**	___	___/___
eek 8	BYE WEEK				
eek 9	**Mon, Nov 4**	**8:15 PM**	**at New York Giants**	___	___/___
eek 10	Sun, Nov 10	8:20 PM	Minnesota Vikings	___	___/___
eek 11	Sun, Nov 17	1:00 PM	at Detroit Lions	___	___/___
eek 12	Sun, Nov 24	4:25 PM	at New England Patriots	___	___/___
eek 13	Thu, Nov. 28	4:30 PM	Buffalo Bills	___	___/___
eek 14	Thu, Dec 5	8:20 PM	at Chicago Bears	___	___/___
eek 15	Sun, Dec 15	4:25 PM	Los Angeles Rams	___	___/___
eek 16	**Sun, Dec 22**	**4:25 PM**	**at Philadelphia Eagles**	___	___/___
eek 17	**Sun, Dec 29**	**1:00 PM**	**Washington Redskins**	___	___/___

END OF SEASON RECORD:___/___

DIVISION TOTAL WIN/LOSS: ___/___

DENVER BRONCOS

Head Coach: Vic Fangio* | 2018 Record: 6-10
First Round Draft Pick: Noah Fant – TE (20)

*new co

John Elway sure *sounds* like he knows what he's doing. And no one can question his skill as a *player*. But are we in "Michael Jordan territory" here — a great player who's not as great running the team as he was running the huddle? We've seen a virtual New-York-subway turnstile at quarterback in the past four years... let's recap: ever since Peyton Manning retired, we've had Brock Osweiler, Trevor Siemian, Paxton Lynch, and Case Keenum. Some of those more than once. And none of those looks destined to become anyone's franchise QB (or even *starting* QB long-term). Elway seems to have conceded that talent-spotting ain't his, well, talent (consider the fact that Denver's best player last year was an *undrafted* free agent) — so Elway's taking a different approach this year by signing veteran QB Joe Flacco. Oh, and by firing head coach Vance Joseph and hiring defense-minded Vic Fangio. Flacco should provide more stability, and we should note that Elway couldn't resist drafting yet another rookie quarterback, this time in the second-round, with Drew Lock; but we're not convinced there's much excitement yet at Mile High Stadium.

DENVER BRONCOS

ep track of wins and losses (division games in bold)				W/L	RUNNING TOTAL
eek 1	Mon, Sep 9	10:20 PM	at Oakland Raiders	___	___/___
eek 2	Sun, Sep 15	4:25 PM	Chicago Bears	___	___/___
eek 3	Sun, Sep 22	1:00 PM	at Green Bay Packers	___	___/___
eek 4	Sun, Sep 29	4:25 PM	Jacksonville Jaguars	___	___/___
eek 5	**Sun, Oct 6**	**4:05 PM**	**at Los Angeles Chargers**	___	___/___
eek 6	Sun, Oct 13	4:25 PM	Tennessee Titans	___	___/___
eek 7	**Thu, Oct 17**	**8:20 PM**	**Kansas City Chiefs**	___	___/___
eek 8	Sun, Oct 27	4:25 PM	at Indianapolis Colts	___	___/___
eek 9	Sun, Nov 3	4:25 PM	Cleveland Browns	___	___/___
eek 10	BYE WEEK				
eek 11	Sun, Nov 17	1:00 PM	at Minnesota Vikings	___	___/___
eek 12	Sun, Nov 24	1:00 PM	at Buffalo Bills	___	___/___
eek 13	**Sun, Dec 1**	**4:25 PM**	**Los Angeles Chargers**	___	___/___
eek 14	Sun, Dec 8	1:00 PM	at Houston Texans	___	___/___
eek 15	**Sun, Dec 15**	**1:00 PM**	**at Kansas City Chiefs**	___	___/___
eek 16	Sun, Dec 22	1:00 PM	Detroit Lions	___	___/___
eek 17	**Sun, Dec 29**	**4:25 PM**	**Oakland Raiders**	___	___/___

END OF SEASON RECORD:___/___

DIVISION TOTAL WIN/LOSS: ___/___

DETROIT LIONS

Head Coach: Matt Patricia | 2018 Record: 6-10
First Round Draft Pick: T.J. Hockenson – TE (8)

2018 wasn't much to write home about. Matt Patricia had trouble getting buy-in from the team on his New England Patriots' style of "do your job" football, and the Lions finished in last place in their division. But some of the malcontents are gone, and the new guys seem more willing to trust Patricia. We're getting a little impatient with Matt Stafford, who seems more interested in record-breaking stats than post-season play, but the selection of what many considered the best tight end in this year's draft should give Stafford a big, strong, reliable receiver who can also block and fight for yards after the catch. Expect the highlight reel from Detroit to feature a lot of names you've never heard of, but fans are still hoping Patricia can bring some Patriots magic to Ford Field.

DETROIT LIONS

TEAM SCHEDULE
Detroit Lions

			ep track of wins and losses **(division games in bold)**	W/L	RUNNING TOTAL
eek 1	Sun, Sep 8	4:25 PM	at Arizona Cardinals	___	___/___
eek 2	Sun, Sep 15	1:00 PM	Los Angeles Chargers	___	___/___
eek 3	Sun, Sep 22	1:00 PM	at Philadelphia Eagles	___	___/___
eek 4	Sun, Sep 29	1:00 PM	Kansas City Chiefs	___	___/___
eek 5	BYE WEEK				
eek 6	**Mon, Oct 14**	**8:15 PM**	**at Green Bay Packers**	___	___/___
eek 7	**Sun, Oct 20**	**1:00 PM**	**Minnesota Vikings**	___	___/___
eek 8	Sun, Oct 27	1:00 PM	New York Giants	___	___/___
eek 9	Sun, Nov 3	4:05 PM	at Oakland Raiders	___	___/___
eek 10	**Sun, Nov 10**	**1:00 PM**	**at Chicago Bears**	___	___/___
eek 11	Sun, Nov 17	1:00 PM	Dallas Cowboys	___	___/___
eek 12	Sun, Nov 24	1:00 PM	at Washington Redskins	___	___/___
eek 13	**Thu, Nov 28**	**12:30 PM**	**Chicago Bears**	___	___/___
eek 14	**Sun, Dec 8**	**1:00 PM**	**at Minnesota Vikings**	___	___/___
eek 15	Sun, Dec 15	1:00 PM	Tampa Bay Buccaneers	___	___/___
eek 16	Sun, Dec 22	1:00 PM	at Denver Broncos	___	___/___
eek 17	**Sun, Dec 29**	**1:00 PM**	**Green Bay Packers**	___	___/___

END OF SEASON RECORD:___/___

DIVISION TOTAL WIN/LOSS: ___/___

GREEN BAY PACKERS

Head Coach: Matt LaFleur* | 2018 Record: 6-9-1

First Round Draft Picks: Rashan Gary – DE (12); Darnell Savage – S (21

*new co

Last year we asked if it really made sense to make Aaron Rodgers unhappy. Half-way through the season, we got the answer: nope. The Packers fired 13-year head coach Mike McCarthy in early December, capping a two-year stretch when the team's superstar quarterback and Super Bowl winning coach just were not on the same page. Enter Matt LaFleur, he of the Sean McVay/ Kyle Shannahan mindset, another young offensive-minded head coach that the NFL is lately so in love with. But is our new buck already butting heads with ARod? Tensions were apparent in the summer, as LaFleur's two-option model seemed bound to hand-cuff one of the smartest, savviest, most resourceful quarterbacks to ever play the game. (Remind us why Green Bay didn't find a defensive guru for head coach, and let Aaron be Aaron?) We like the two defensive players taken in the first round, but with Rodgers and LaFleur potentially battling for control of the offense, we are worried this might be a bumpy transition.

GREEN BAY PACKERS

TEAM SCHEDULE
Green Bay Packers

				W/L	RUNNING TOTAL
ep track of wins and losses (division games in bold)					
eek 1	**Thu, Sep 5**	**8:20 PM**	**at Chicago Bears**	___	___/___
eek 2	**Sun, Sep 15**	**1:00 PM**	**Minnesota Vikings**	___	___/___
eek 3	Sun, Sep 22	1:00 PM	Denver Broncos	___	___/___
eek 4	Thu, Sep 26	8:20 PM	Philadelphia Eagles	___	___/___
eek 5	Sun, Oct 6	4:25 PM	at Dallas Cowboys	___	___/___
eek 6	**Mon, Oct 14**	**8:15 PM**	**Detroit Lions**	___	___/___
eek 7	Sun, Oct 20	1:00 PM	Oakland Raiders	___	___/___
eek 8	Sun, Oct 27	8:20 PM	at Kansas City Chiefs	___	___/___
eek 9	Sun, Nov 3	4:25 PM	at Los Angeles Chargers	___	___/___
eek 10	Sun, Nov 10	1:00 PM	Carolina Panthers	___	___/___
eek 11	BYE WEEK				
eek 12	Sun, Nov 24	4:25 PM	at San Francisco 49ers	___	___/___
eek 13	Sun, Dec 1	1:00 PM	at New York Giants	___	___/___
eek 14	Sun, Dec 8	1:00 PM	Washington Redskins	___	___/___
eek 15	**Sun, Dec 15**	**1:00 PM**	**Chicago Bears**	___	___/___
eek 16	**Mon, Dec 23**	**8:15 PM**	**at Minnesota Vikings**	___	___/___
eek 17	**Sun, Dec 29**	**1:00 PM**	**at Detroit Lions**	___	___/___

END OF SEASON RECORD:___/___

DIVISION TOTAL WIN/LOSS: ___/___

HOUSTON TEXANS

Head Coach: Bill O'Brien | 2018 Record: 11-5
First Round Draft Pick: Titus Howard - T (23)

Deshaun Watson was back — and so were the Houston Texans. Watson proved his 2017 (pre-injury) brilliance was not a case of beginner's luck, as the Texans jumped back to the top of the AFC South, despite an impressive rebound by the Colts. The biggest question mark was, however, protecting their future franchise QB, and so Houston had their sights set on the outstanding tackle Andre Dillard in the draft. But so did Philadelphia, who jumped ahead of Houston to take Dillard at #22, forcing the Texans to go with their second-choice, tackle Titus Howard. Now we have to hope they didn't reach. The Texans welcome back stars on both sides of the ball - wide receiver Deandre Hopkins looks to be one of the top five receivers in the league (only Julio Jones had more receiving yards in 2018), while J.J. Watt (behind only Aaron Donald for most sacks last year) and Jadaveon Clowney both had exceptional play in 2018. Note: Clowney was franchise-tagged for 2019, so the Texans may decide to trade him, but we hope he stays — and plays — for at least one more year. With all this talent, Houston is set to make a much deeper run into the playoffs. And if they don't, questions will start to surface about the head coach.

HOUSTON TEXANS

TEAM SCHEDULE
Houston Texans

				W/L	RUNNING TOTAL
*ep track of wins and losses (**division games in bold**)					
eek 1	Mon, Sep 9	7:10 PM	at New Orleans Saints	___	___/___
eek 2	**Sun, Sep 15**	**1:00 PM**	**Jacksonville Jaguars**	___	___/___
eek 3	Sun, Sep 22	4:25 PM	at Los Angeles Chargers	___	___/___
eek 4	Sun, Sep 29	1:00 PM	Carolina Panthers	___	___/___
eek 5	Sun, Oct 6	1:00 PM	Atlanta Falcons	___	___/___
eek 6	Sun, Oct 13	1:00 PM	at Kansas City Chiefs	___	___/___
eek 7	**Sun, Oct 20**	**1:00 PM**	**at Indianapolis Colts**	___	___/___
eek 8	Sun, Oct 27	1:00 PM	Oakland Raiders	___	___/___
eek 9	**Sun, Nov 3**	**9:30 AM**	**at Jacksonville Jaguars**	___	___/___
eek 10	BYE WEEK				
eek 11	Sun, Nov 17	1:00 PM	at Baltimore Ravens	___	___/___
eek 12	**Thu, Nov 21**	**8:20 PM**	**Indianapolis Colts**	___	___/___
eek 13	Sun, Dec 1	8:20 PM	New England Patriots	___	___/___
eek 14	Sun, Dec 8	1:00 PM	Denver Broncos	___	___/___
eek 15	**Sun, Dec 15**	**1:00 PM**	**at Tennessee Titans**	___	___/___
eek 16	Sun, Dec 22	1:00 PM	at Tampa Bay Buccaneers	___	___/___
eek 17	**Sun, Dec 29**	**1:00 PM**	**Tennessee Titans**	___	___/___

END OF SEASON RECORD:___/___

DIVISION TOTAL WIN/LOSS: ___/___

Andrew Luck was the 2018 comeback player of the year, and boy, did he ever come back. Throwing 39 touchdowns and nearly 4,600 yards, and leading his team to a top-five rank in points per game, Luck proved he has fully healed and is ready to take his place among the league's elite QB's. The Colt's first-round pick, Quenton Nelson, proved his worth, as a key piece of a significantly better offensive line (*see "4,600 yards" above*). And Indy's defense was also much-improved in 2018, with Darius Leonard leading the league in tackles. Honestly, if Matt Nagy hadn't won, Frank Reich was the other first-year head-coach to deserve coach-of-the-year honors. As we head into 2019, the biggest hole might still be at receiver — Luck is the classic pocket passer, and he needs someone to pass to. T.Y Hilton is great, but Luck needs more targets, and Indy is hoping their second-round pick Parris Campbell (who many projected to be a first-round talent), will provide another play-maker for the Colts.

INDIANAPOLIS COLTS

TEAM SCHEDULE
Indianapolis Colts

				RUNNING
ep track of wins and losses (division games in bold)			W/L	TOTAL
eek 1	Sun, Sep 8	4:05 PM	at Los Angeles Chargers	___	___/___
eek 2	**Sun, Sep 15**	**1:00 PM**	**at Tennessee Titans**	**___**	**___/___**
eek 3	Sun, Sep 22	1:00 PM	Atlanta Falcons	___	___/___
eek 4	Sun, Sep 29	1:00 PM	Oakland Raiders	___	___/___
eek 5	Sun, Oct 6	8:20 PM	at Kansas City Chiefs	___	___/___
eek 6	BYE WEEK				
eek 7	**Sun, Oct 20**	**1:00 PM**	**Houston Texans**	**___**	**___/___**
eek 8	Sun, Oct 27	4:25 PM	Denver Broncos	___	___/___
eek 9	Sun, Nov 3	1:00 PM	at Pittsburgh Steelers	___	___/___
eek 10	Sun, Nov 10	4:05 PM	Miami Dolphins	___	___/___
eek 11	**Sun, Nov 17**	**1:00 PM**	**Jacksonville Jaguars**	**___**	**___/___**
eek 12	**Thu, Nov 21**	**8:20 PM**	**at Houston Texans**	**___**	**___/___**
eek 13	**Sun, Dec 1**	**1:00 PM**	**Tennessee Titans**	**___**	**___/___**
eek 14	Sun, Dec 8	1:00 PM	at Tampa Bay Buccaneers	___	___/___
eek 15	Mon, Dec 16	8:15 PM	at New Orleans Saints	___	___/___
eek 16	Sun, Dec 22	1:00 PM	Carolina Panthers	___	___/___
eek 17	**Sun, Dec 29**	**1:00 PM**	**at Jacksonville Jaguars**	**___**	**___/___**

END OF SEASON RECORD:___/___

DIVISION TOTAL WIN/LOSS: ___/___

JACKSONVILLE JAGUARS

Head Coach: Doug Marrone | 2018 Record: 5-11
First Round Draft Pick: Josh Allen – DE (7)

The Jaguars have finally moved on from Blake Bortles, and fans are excited about their new quarterback. After all, who wouldn't want a recent Super Bowl MVP? Welcome to Florida, Nick Foles, you've earned your place as a proven starter. The only thing that can stop you is yourself. Doug Marrone and Tom Coughlin seem a good pair to help Foles be his best, but Jacksonville may be losing patience with this leadership team. After coming so close to the Super Bowl in 2017, the Jaguars had a very poor year in 2018, and Jags fans have high expectations for a bounce-back year. The defense needs to play up to their talent, which includes Calais Campbell, Jalen Ramsey and A. J. Bouye — but the real question remains on offense. The Jags drafted tight end Josh Oliver in round three, and signed two free agency receivers in Chris Conley (WR) and Geoff Swaim (TE). If all these new players can gel — and we get the best of RB Leonard Fournette, Nick Foles might just have enough pieces to take his new team back to the playoffs.

JACKSONVILLE JAGUARS

TEAM SCHEDULE
Jacksonville Jaguars

...ep track of wins and losses (*division games in bold*)				W/L	RUNNING TOTAL
...eek 1	Sun, Sep 8	1:00 PM	Kansas City Chiefs	___	___/___
...eek 2	**Sun, Sep 15**	**1:00 PM**	**at Houston Texans**	___	___/___
...eek 3	**Thu, Sep 19**	**8:20 PM**	**Tennessee Titans**	___	___/___
...eek 4	Sun, Sep 29	4:25 PM	at Denver Broncos	___	___/___
...eek 5	Sun, Oct 6	1:00 PM	at Carolina Panthers	___	___/___
...eek 6	Sun, Oct 13	1:00 PM	New Orleans Saints	___	___/___
...eek 7	Sun, Oct 20	1:00 PM	at Cincinnati Bengals	___	___/___
...eek 8	Sun, Oct 27	1:00 PM	New York Jets	___	___/___
...eek 9	**Sun, Nov 3**	**9:30 AM**	**Houston Texans**	___	___/___
...eek 10	BYE WEEK				
...eek 11	**Sun, Nov 17**	**1:00 PM**	**at Indianapolis Colts**	___	___/___
...eek 12	**Sun, Nov 24**	**4:05 PM**	**at Tennessee Titans**	___	___/___
...eek 13	Sun, Dec 1	1:00 PM	Tampa Bay Buccaneers	___	___/___
...eek 14	Sun, Dec 8	4:05 PM	Los Angeles Chargers	___	___/___
...eek 15	Sun, Dec 15	4:05 PM	at Oakland Raiders	___	___/___
...eek 16	Sun, Dec 22	1:00 PM	at Atlanta Falcons	___	___/___
...eek 17	**Sun, Dec 29**	**1:00 PM**	**Indianapolis Colts**	___	___/___

END OF SEASON RECORD:___/___

DIVISION TOTAL WIN/LOSS: ___/___

KANSAS CITY CHIEFS

Head Coach: Andy Reid | 2018 Record: 12-4
First Round Draft Pick: No Picks in Round 1

Another great year for Andy Reid's Chiefs, and yet, another disappointing ending. For most of the season, the story was the sensational play of second-year QB Patrick Mahomes, proving Andy Reid right when he traded away Alex Smith to place his bet on Mahomes. Excellent decision, Andy — Mahomes was lights out, thrilling fans with his skill set (did you prefer the left-handed pass or the no-look pass?), on his way to throwing for more than 5,000 yards and winning MVP of the league. So, Kansas City has their franchise quarterback, terrific. But they lost one star player to scandal mid-season (Kareem Hunt) and are in danger of losing another one to yet another scandal (Tyreek Hill). Both those players were exceptional, and it's not easy to replace exceptional. Meanwhile, this team's Achilles heel is still their defense, which ranked second-to-*last* in yards allowed per game, despite the outstanding play of Chris Jones, who racked up 15.5 sacks. We are not huge Steve Spagnola fans, and while we love Patty Mahomes, we are still a bit worried about the rest of the picture.

KANSAS CITY CHIEFS

TEAM SCHEDULE
Kansas City Chiefs

...ep track of wins and losses **(division games in bold)**				W/L	RUNNING TOTAL
...eek 1	Sun, Sep 8	1:00 PM	at Jacksonville Jaguars	___	___/___
...eek 2	**Sun, Sep 15**	**4:05 PM**	**at Oakland Raiders**	___	___/___
...eek 3	Sun, Sep 22	1:00 PM	Baltimore Ravens	___	___/___
...eek 4	Sun, Sep 29	1:00 PM	at Detroit Lions	___	___/___
...eek 5	Sun, Oct 6	8:20 PM	Indianapolis Colts	___	___/___
...eek 6	Sun, Oct 13	1:00 PM	Houston Texans	___	___/___
...eek 7	**Thu, Oct 17**	**8:20 PM**	**at Denver Broncos**	___	___/___
...eek 8	Sun, Oct 27	8:20 PM	Green Bay Packers	___	___/___
...eek 9	Sun, Nov 3	1:00 PM	Minnesota Vikings	___	___/___
...eek 10	Sun, Nov 10	1:00 PM	at Tennessee Titans	___	___/___
...eek 11	**Mon, Nov 18**	**8:15 PM**	**at Los Angeles Chargers**	___	___/___
...eek 12	BYE WEEK				
...eek 13	**Sun, Dec. 1**	**1:00 PM**	**Oakland Raiders**	___	___/___
...eek 14	Sun, Dec 8	4:25 PM	at New England Patriots	___	___/___
...eek 15	**Sun, Dec 15**	**1:00 PM**	**Denver Broncos**	___	___/___
...eek 16	Sun, Dec 22	8:20 PM	at Chicago Bears	___	___/___
...eek 17	**Sun, Dec 29**	**1:00 PM**	**Los Angeles Chargers**	___	___/___

END OF SEASON RECORD:___/___

DIVISION TOTAL WIN/LOSS: ___/___

LOS ANGELES CHARGERS

Head Coach: Anthony Lynn | 2018 Record: 12-4
First Round Draft Pick: Jerry Tillery – DT (28)

The LA Chargers were sneaky good last year, and with Philip Rivers staying healthy, they almost overtook Kansas City to win the AFC West. They beat the Ravens in round one of the playoffs, but lost to the Patriots in the Divisional Round, and were home once again to watch the AFC Championship Game. Keenan Allen, Melvin Gordon, Austin Eckler — all three had excellent performance in 2018, and all three are back for the 2019 season. Add in the resurgent Mike Williams, and the outstanding young tight end Hunter Henry, and the offense looks potent once again. On the defensive side, Joey Bosa is the defense's poster boy, and rookie Derwin James had a terrific year, so the arrow is definitely pointing up on him. Chargers' first-round pick Jerry Tillery was rated a "steal" at #28, and many experts list the Chargers as one of the most talented and well-rounded teams in the NFL. We'd love to see Rivers get to the big dance before he retires, but how many more years can he possibly have left? Cynics have begun the look-out for Father Time.

LOS ANGELES CHARGERS

TEAM SCHEDULE
Los Angeles Chargers

				W/L	RUNNING TOTAL
ep track of wins and losses **(division games in bold)**					
eek 1	Sun, Sep 8	4:05 PM	Indianapolis Colts	___	___/___
eek 2	Sun, Sep 15	1:00 PM	at Detroit Lions	___	___/___
eek 3	Sun, Sep 22	4:25 PM	Houston Texans	___	___/___
eek 4	Sun, Sep 29	1:00 PM	at Miami Dolphins	___	___/___
eek 5	**Sun, Oct 6**	**4:05 PM**	**Denver Broncos**	___	___/___
eek 6	Sun, Oct 13	8:20 PM	Pittsburgh Steelers	___	___/___
eek 7	Sun, Oct 20	4:05 PM	at Tennessee Titans	___	___/___
eek 8	Sun, Oct 27	1:00 PM	at Chicago Bears	___	___/___
eek 9	Sun, Nov 3	4:25 PM	Green Bay Packers	___	___/___
eek 10	**Thu, Nov 7**	**8:20 PM**	**at Oakland Raiders**	___	___/___
eek 11	**Mon, Nov 18**	**8:15 PM**	**Kansas City Chiefs**	___	___/___
eek 12	BYE WEEK				
eek 13	**Sun, Dec 1**	**4:25 PM**	**at Denver Broncos**	___	___/___
eek 14	Sun, Dec 8	4:05 PM	at Jacksonville Jaguars	___	___/___
eek 15	Sun, Dec 15	8:20 PM	Minnesota Vikings	___	___/___
eek 16	**Sun, Dec 22**	**1:00 PM**	**Oakland Raiders**	___	___/___
eek 17	**Sun, Dec 29**	**1:00 PM**	**at Kansas City Chiefs**	___	___/___

END OF SEASON RECORD:___/___

DIVISION TOTAL WIN/LOSS: ___/___

LOS ANGELES RAMS

Head Coach: Sean McVay | 2018 Record: 13-3
First Round Draft Pick: Traded Pick #31 to Atlanta

The Rams proved they were for real last season, making it all the way to the SuperBowl before wilting under the power of the G.O.A.T. Sean McVay had a win-now attitude all year, spending big money on short-term "rentals" like Ndamukong Suh, to add to an already stacked defense that includes Aaron Donald, Marcus Peters, and Aqib Talib, while Jared Goff and Todd Gurley both had top-five performances in passing and rushing, respectively. Goff doubters were silenced (at least temporarily), and the team as a whole moved through the NFC like a well-oiled machine, earning top-five team stats for points per game, yards per game, and interceptions per year. If you thought the Rams were strong defensively last year, consider they added Clay Matthews and Eric Weddle this off-season — and may only lose Suh of the names listed here. Where they did suffer some erosion, though, was on the offensive line- and that could be a problem for Goff, who isn't as much of a scrambler as fellow young star QBs Watson, Wentz, Mahomes and Mayfield. Still, this team is built to make the playoffs, and has the coach to take them back there.

LOS ANGELES RAMS

TEAM SCHEDULE
Los Angeles Rams

ep track of wins and losses (division games in bold)				W/L	RUNNING TOTAL
eek 1	Sun, Sep 8	1:00 PM	at Carolina Panthers	___	___/___
eek 2	Sun, Sep 15	4:25 PM	New Orleans Saints	___	___/___
eek 3	Sun, Sep 22	8:20 PM	at Cleveland Browns	___	___/___
eek 4	Sun, Sep 29	4:05 PM	Tampa Bay Buccaneers	___	___/___
eek 5	**Thu, Oct 3**	**8:20 PM**	**at Seattle Seahawks**	___	___/___
eek 6	**Sun, Oct 13**	**4:05 PM**	**San Francisco 49ers**	___	___/___
eek 7	Sun, Oct 20	1:00 PM	at Atlanta Falcons	___	___/___
eek 8	Sun, Oct 27	1:00 PM	Cincinnati Bengals	___	___/___
eek 9	BYE WEEK				
eek 10	Sun, Nov 10	4:25 PM	at Pittsburgh Steelers	___	___/___
eek 11	Sun, Nov 17	8:20 PM	Chicago Bears	___	___/___
eek 12	Mon, Nov 25	8:15 PM	Baltimore Ravens	___	___/___
eek 13	**Sun, Dec 1**	**4:05 PM**	**at Arizona Cardinals**	___	___/___
eek 14	**Sun, Dec 8**	**8:20 PM**	**Seattle Seahawks**	___	___/___
eek 15	Sun, Dec 15	4:25 PM	at Dallas Cowboys	___	___/___
eek 16	**Sun, Dec 22**	**1:00 PM**	**at San Francisco 49ers**	___	___/___
eek 17	**Sun, Dec 29**	**4:25 PM**	**Arizona Cardinals**	___	___/___

END OF SEASON RECORD:___/___

DIVISION TOTAL WIN/LOSS: ___/___

MIAMI DOLPHINS

Head Coach: Brian Flores* | 2018 Record: 7-9
First Round Draft Pick: Christian Wilkins – DT (13)

*new coa

Miami went in the wrong direction in 2018, and Head Coach Adam Gase paid the price. Their only real bright spot was intercepting the ball, led by Xavien Howard — but the Dolphins were bottom-five in defending the run and overall yards allowed per game. To make matters worse, QB Ryan Tannehill had no "come-back" year, and the offense turned in a disappointing near-last-place finish in total yards per game. But buckle up for a whole lotta new, as Miami not only hired a new head coach, they brought in a new last-year's-rookie quarterback. Odd man out at Arizona, Josh Rosen needed a fresh start, and Miami needed a reset at QB. So Miami pulled off a neat draft-weekend trade, forcing Arizona to accept a second-round pick in exchange for the QB they drafted at #10 overall just one year earlier. (To add insult to injury, Miami *traded down* that second-round pick before trading it away to Arizona.) But after that dust settled, the important question remains: does Josh Rosen have what it takes to succeed as a starting QB in the NFL? Hard to tell after getting beat up in Arizona, but this year we should be able to answer that question — especially with a new head-coach from the Bill Belichick tree. Dolphin fans are hoping they hooked a prize fish.

MIAMI DOLPHINS

TEAM SCHEDULE
Miami Dolphins

				W/L	RUNNING TOTAL
...ep track of wins and losses **(division games in bold)**					
eek 1	Sun, Sep 8	1:00 PM	Baltimore Ravens	___	___/___
eek 2	**Sun, Sep 15**	**1:00 PM**	**New England Patriots**	___	___/___
eek 3	Sun, Sep 22	1:00 PM	at Dallas Cowboys	___	___/___
eek 4	Sun, Sep 29	1:00 PM	Los Angeles Chargers	___	___/___
eek 5	BYE WEEK				
eek 6	Sun, Oct 13	1:00 PM	Washington Redskins	___	___/___
eek 7	**Sun, Oct 20**	**1:00 PM**	**at Buffalo Bills**	___	___/___
eek 8	Mon, Oct 28	8:15 PM	at Pittsburgh Steelers	___	___/___
eek 9	**Sun, Nov. 3**	**1:00 PM**	**New York Jets**	___	___/___
eek 10	Sun, Nov 10	4:05 PM	at Indianapolis Colts	___	___/___
eek 11	**Sun, Nov 17**	**1:00 PM**	**Buffalo Bills**	___	___/___
eek 12	Sun, Nov 24	1:00 PM	at Cleveland Browns	___	___/___
eek 13	Sun, Dec 1	1:00 PM	Philadelphia Eagles	___	___/___
eek 14	**Sun, Dec 8**	**1:00 PM**	**at New York Jets**	___	___/___
eek 15	Sun, Dec 15	1:00 PM	at New York Giants	___	___/___
eek 16	Sun, Dec 22	1:00 PM	Cincinnati Bengals	___	___/___
eek 17	**Sun, Dec 29**	**1:00 PM**	**at New England Patriots**	___	___/___

END OF SEASON RECORD:___/___

DIVISION TOTAL WIN/LOSS: ___/___

MINNESOTA VIKINGS

Head Coach: Mike Zimmer | 2018 Record: 8-7-1
First Round Draft Pick: Garret Bradbury - C (18)

Kirk Cousins wasn't bad, really he wasn't — but living up to that giant, $84-million-guaranteed contract was going to require exceptional play, and exceptional he was not. Despite having one of the NFL's most talented and exciting receiving duos in Stefon Diggs and Adam Thielen, Cousins did not produce magic — partly due to the weakness of his interior offensive line. Meanwhile, Mike Zimmer got so fed up with his offensive coordinator John DeFilippo that he fired him mid-way through the season. The Vikings looked to attack their O-line weakness head-on, by taking center Garret Bradbury in the first round, and Bradbury looks likely to start early and play often this season. Whether that will be the key to unlocking championship play for Cousins remains to be seen. But we like the move to cement Kevin Stefanski as offensive coordinator, and we expect Minnesota to compete once again for the division in 2019.

MINNESOTA VIKINGS

TEAM SCHEDULE
Minnesota Vikings

ep track of wins and losses *(division games in bold)*

				W/L	RUNNING TOTAL
eek 1	Sun, Sep 8	1:00 PM	Atlanta Falcons	___	___/___
eek 2	**Sun, Sep 15**	**1:00 PM**	**at Green Bay Packers**	___	___/___
eek 3	Sun, Sep 22	1:00 PM	Oakland Raiders	___	___/___
eek 4	**Sun, Sep 29**	**4:25 PM**	**at Chicago Bears**	___	___/___
eek 5	Sun, Oct 6	1:00 PM	at New York Giants	___	___/___
eek 6	Sun, Oct 13	1:00 PM	Philadelphia Eagles	___	___/___
eek 7	**Sun, Oct 20**	**1:00 PM**	**at Detroit Lions**	___	___/___
eek 8	Thu, Oct 24	8:20 PM	Washington Redskins	___	___/___
eek 9	Sun, Nov 3	1:00 PM	at Kansas City Chiefs	___	___/___
eek 10	Sun, Nov 10	8:20 PM	at Dallas Cowboys	___	___/___
eek 11	Sun, Nov 17	1:00 PM	Denver Broncos	___	___/___
eek 12	BYE WEEK				
eek 13	Mon, Dec 2	8:15 PM	at Seattle Seahawks	___	___/___
eek 14	**Sun, Dec 8**	**1:00 PM**	**Detroit Lions**	___	___/___
eek 15	Sun, Dec 15	8:20 PM	at Los Angeles Chargers	___	___/___
eek 16	**Mon, Dec 23**	**8:15 PM**	**Green Bay Packers**	___	___/___
eek 17	**Sun, Dec 29**	**1:00 PM**	**Chicago Bears**	___	___/___

END OF SEASON RECORD:___/___

DIVISION TOTAL WIN/LOSS: ___/___

NEW ENGLAND PATRIOTS

Head Coach: Bill Belichick | 2018 Record: 11-5
First Round Draft Pick: N'Keal Harry - WR (32)

Honestly, this is getting a little boring. With apologies to all my friends and family in New England, aren't we ready for someone else, *anyone else*, to win the AFC — not to mention, the Super Bowl? But Belichick and Brady did it again, hoisting the Lombardi trophy for a remarkable six times in the Brady-Belichick era. Edelman was great, Gronk was great, Brady was great, yada, yada, yada. But for the first time in a very long time, the lead story for 2019 is not the return of Brady; it's the retirement of Rob Gronkowski. The Pats' star tight end was so clutch, this will be a new look without him. New England, of course, was focused on business — and drafted a big, strong wide receiver in the first round, no doubt to fill, at least in part, Gronk's very large shoes. They also signed veteran tight end Ben Watson, but he may be out for the first four games of the season on a technicality (we'd call it that — he thought he had retired, after all). No smart money ever counts out New England; as long as they have Brady and Belichick, they are favorites to win the AFC. Yep, again.

NEW ENGLAND PATRIOTS

New England Patriots

					RUNNING
ep track of wins and losses **(division games in bold)**				W/L	TOTAL
eek 1	Sun, Sep 8	8:20 PM	Pittsburgh Steelers	___	__/__
eek 2	**Sun, Sep 15**	**1:00 PM**	**at Miami Dolphins**	___	__/__
eek 3	**Sun, Sep 22**	**1:00 PM**	**New York Jets**	___	__/__
eek 4	**Sun, Sep 29**	**1:00 PM**	**at Buffalo Bills**	___	__/__
eek 5	Sun, Oct 6	1:00 PM	at Washington Redskins	___	__/__
eek 6	Thu, Oct 10	8:20 PM	New York Giants	___	__/__
eek 7	**Mon, Oct 21**	**8:15 PM**	**at New York Jets**	___	__/__
eek 8	Sun, Oct 27	4:25 PM	Cleveland Browns	___	__/__
eek 9	Sun, Nov 3	8:20 PM	at Baltimore Ravens	___	__/__
eek 10	BYE WEEK				
eek 11	Sun, Nov 17	4:25 PM	at Philadelphia Eagles	___	__/__
eek 12	Sun, Nov 24	4:25 PM	Dallas Cowboys	___	__/__
eek 13	Sun, Dec 1	8:20 PM	at Houston Texans	___	__/__
eek 14	Sun, Dec 8	4:25 PM	Kansas City Chiefs	___	__/__
eek 15	Sun, Dec 15	1:00 PM	at Cincinnati Bengals	___	__/__
eek 16	**Sun, Dec 22**	**1:00 PM**	**Buffalo Bills**	___	__/__
eek 17	**Sun, Dec 29**	**1:00 PM**	**Miami Dolphins**	___	__/__

END OF SEASON RECORD:__/__

DIVISION TOTAL WIN/LOSS: __/__

NEW ORLEANS SAINTS

Head Coach: Sean Payton | 2018 Record: 13-3
First Round Draft Pick: No Picks in Round 1

Heart-breaking doesn't even begin to cover it. I mean, it was bad enough to lose in 2017 on a miraculous play by the Minnesota Vikings — but to get all the way back to the NFC Championship only to have the ref watch Rams' cornerback Nickell Robey-Coleman chuck Stefon Diggs out of bounds and not call a foul? Seriously, that's hard to swallow. It was the story of the play-offs, and led to a change in the pass interference rules and the way coaches and refs can review calls (and non-calls). But all that didn't matter in January, when the Saints had to pick up their marbles and go home. Take a deep breath, and start over. New Orleans still has one of the best quarterbacks to ever play the position in Drew Brees, and one of the best coaches in the league in Sean Payton. The Saints have added tight end Jared Cook and running back Latavius Murray, to an offense that also includes the young star rusher Alvin Kamara. But losing Mark Ingram is tough, and Payton will have to get creative to match last year's production (when the Saints ranked behind only the Chiefs and the Rams in points per game). We just hope Drew Brees gets another chance at the Super Bowl — perhaps the third time is the charm?

NEW ORLEANS SAINTS

TEAM SCHEDULE
New Orleans Saints

ep track of wins and losses *(division games in bold)*

				W/L	RUNNING TOTAL
eek 1	Mon, Sep 9	7:10 PM	Houston Texans	___	___/___
eek 2	Sun, Sep 15	4:25 PM	at Los Angeles Rams	___	___/___
eek 3	Sun, Sep 22	4:25 PM	at Seattle Seahawks	___	___/___
eek 4	Sun, Sep 29	8:20 PM	Dallas Cowboys	___	___/___
eek 5	**Sun, Oct 6**	**1:00 PM**	**Tampa Bay Buccaneers**	___	___/___
eek 6	Sun, Oct 13	1:00 PM	at Jacksonville Jaguars	___	___/___
eek 7	Sun, Oct 20	4:25 PM	at Chicago Bears	___	___/___
eek 8	Sun, Oct 27	1:00 PM	Arizona Cardinals	___	___/___
eek 9	BYE WEEK				
Week 10	**Sun, Nov 10**	**1:00 PM**	**Atlanta Falcons**	___	___/___
Week 11	**Sun, Nov 17**	**1:00 PM**	**at Tampa Bay Buccaneers**	___	___/___
Week 12	**Sun, Nov 24**	**1:00 PM**	**Carolina Panthers**	___	___/___
Week 13	**Thu, Nov 28**	**8:20 PM**	**at Atlanta Falcons**	___	___/___
Week 14	Sun, Dec 8	1:00 PM	San Francisco 49ers	___	___/___
Week 15	Mon, Dec 16	8:15 PM	Indianapolis Colts	___	___/___
Week 16	Sun, Dec 22	1:00 PM	at Tennessee Titans	___	___/___
Week 17	**Sun, Dec 29**	**1:00 PM**	**at Carolina Panthers**	___	___/___

END OF SEASON RECORD:___/___

DIVISION TOTAL WIN/LOSS: ___/___

NEW YORK GIANTS

Head Coach: Pat Schurmur | 2018 Record: 5-11
First Round Draft Picks: Daniel Jones – QB (6);
Dexter Lawrence – DT (17); DeAndre Baker – CB (26)

There's been a lot of grumbling in New York. Using last year's #2 pick on not-a-quarterback? Trading OBJ? And drafting Daniel Jones? I mean, *Daniel Jones*? No one in the media had Jones as one of the top QB picks, but Shurmur and Gettleman clearly don't care about what "the experts" say. Saquon Barkley was, indeed, an exceptional RB, worthy of his first-round pick (second only to Zeke Elliott in total rushing yards for the season). And Jones had the Manning blessing, so he's the man they picked to take over once the Eli era is over. And when will that be, you ask? Could be soon, quite soon. Jones' college resume was not overwhelming, but early reports this summer suggest he may be better than advertised. Giants fans certainly hope so, as Eli seems to have passed his prime — and without Beckham, this offense is in dire need of receivers. We like Golden Tate, but no way is he replacing the production of Odell, and we are not picking the Giants to win this division in 2019.

NEW YORK GIANTS

TEAM SCHEDULE
New York Giants

ep track of wins and losses *(division games in bold)*				W/L	RUNNING TOTAL
eek 1	Sun, Sep 8	4:25 PM	**at Dallas Cowboys**	___	___/___
eek 2	Sun, Sep 15	1:00 PM	Buffalo Bills	___	___/___
eek 3	Sun, Sep 22	4:05 PM	at Tampa Bay Buccaneers	___	___/___
eek 4	**Sun, Sep 29**	**1:00 PM**	**Washington Redskins**	___	___/___
eek 5	Sun, Oct 6	1:00 PM	Minnesota Vikings	___	___/___
eek 6	Thu, Oct 10	8:20 PM	at New England Patriots	___	___/___
eek 7	Sun, Oct 20	1:00 PM	Arizona Cardinals	___	___/___
eek 8	Sun, Oct 27	1:00 PM	at Detroit Lions	___	___/___
eek 9	**Mon, Nov 4**	**8:15 PM**	**Dallas Cowboys**	___	___/___
eek 10	Sun, Nov 10	1:00 PM	at New York Jets	___	___/___
eek 11	BYE WEEK				
eek 12	Sun, Nov 24	1:00 PM	at Chicago Bears	___	___/___
eek 13	Sun, Dec 1	1:00 PM	Green Bay Packers	___	___/___
eek 14	**Mon, Dec 9**	**8:15 PM**	**at Philadelphia Eagles**	___	___/___
eek 15	Sun, Dec 15	1:00 PM	Miami Dolphins	___	___/___
eek 16	**Sat, Dec 22**	**1:00 PM**	**at Washington Redskins**	___	___/___
eek 17	**Sun, Dec 29**	**1:00 PM**	**Philadelphia Eagles**	___	___/___

END OF SEASON RECORD: ___/___

DIVISION TOTAL WIN/LOSS: ___/___

NEW YORK JETS

Head Coach: Adam Gase* | 2018 Record: 4-12
First Round Draft Pick: Quinnen Williams – DT (3)

*new coa

Adam Gase wasn't out of work for long. Soon after being shown the door in Miami, he was scooped up by the Jets to take over after the firing of Todd Bowles. And it's certainly an advantage that Gase has been in the AFC East for the past three years. He should be able to help the Jets get the best of Miami — and he's had time to study the juggernaut that is the New England Patriots. But the Jets are still... a project. We like QB Sam Darnold, and expect him to improve in his second season. And the Jets were thrilled to get Quinnen Williams at #3 to help beef up their defensive line. But the big news in New York is the signing of superstar running back Le'Veon Bell, who sat out all of 2018 rather than play on the franchise tag with the Steelers. They also added Jamison Crowder, a very good receiver from the Redskins. That's not all — the Jets also signed a star on the defense, with C.J. Mosely getting a giant contract to come to New York. We like these new pieces, and if Darnold steps up, the best New York team this year might just be wearing green.

NEW YORK JETS

TEAM SCHEDULE
New York Jets

...ep track of wins and losses (*division games in bold*)				W/L	RUNNING TOTAL
eek 1	**Sun, Sep 8**	**1:00 PM**	**Buffalo Bills**	___	___/___
eek 2	Mon, Sep 16	8:15 PM	Cleveland Browns	___	___/___
eek 3	**Sun, Sep 22**	**1:00 PM**	**at New England Patriots**	___	___/___
eek 4	BYE WEEK				
eek 5	Sun, Oct 6	1:00 PM	at Philadelphia Eagles	___	___/___
eek 6	Sun, Oct 13	4:25 PM	Dallas Cowboys	___	___/___
eek 7	**Mon, Oct 21**	**8:15 PM**	**New England Patriots**	___	___/___
eek 8	Sun, Oct 27	1:00 PM	at Jacksonville Jaguars	___	___/___
eek 9	**Sun, Nov 3**	**1:00 PM**	**at Miami Dolphins**	___	___/___
eek 10	Sun, Nov 10	1:00 PM	New York Giants	___	___/___
eek 11	Sun, Nov 17	1:00 PM	at Washington Redskins	___	___/___
eek 12	Sun, Nov 24	1:00 PM	Oakland Raiders	___	___/___
eek 13	Sun, Dec 1	1:00 PM	at Cincinnati Bengals	___	___/___
eek 14	**Sun, Dec 8**	**1:00 PM**	**Miami Dolphins**	___	___/___
eek 15	Thu, Dec 12	8:20 PM	at Baltimore Ravens	___	___/___
eek 16	Sun, Dec 22	1:00 PM	Pittsburgh Steelers	___	___/___
eek 17	**Sun, Dec 29**	**1:00 PM**	**at Buffalo Bills**	___	___/___

END OF SEASON RECORD:___/___

DIVISION TOTAL WIN/LOSS: ___/___

OAKLAND RAIDERS

Head Coach: Jon Gruden | 2018 Record: 4-12
First Round Draft Picks: Clelin Ferrell – DE (4); Josh Jacobs – RB (24)
Jonathan Abrams – S (27)

Clearly 2018 was a forfeited season. First trading away the best player on the team (Mack), then trading away the best (only good?) receiver Amari Cooper, it just didn't seem like there was a plan (even a will) to win. But Grudin was stockpiling draft picks and looking at the long-term. We like their picks — three in the first round! — but this is still a real work in progress. Grudin and GM Mike Mayock also added talent in free agency, including WR Antonio Brown and LB Vontaze Burfict. Apparently character was not a criterion for the Raiders. We're still not convinced Grudin can pull this off, but we have to admit they have significantly upgraded their roster for 2019. Plus, we want to be a fly on the wall when Gruden reads Antonio Brown the riot act.

OAKLAND RAIDERS

TEAM SCHEDULE
Oakland Raiders

				W/L	RUNNING TOTAL
*ep track of wins and losses **(division games in bold)***					
eek 1	**Mon, Sep 9**	**10:20 PM**	**Denver Broncos**	___	___/___
eek 2	**Sun, Sep 15**	**4:05 PM**	**Kansas City Chiefs**	___	___/___
eek 3	Sun, Sep 22	1:00 PM	at Minnesota Vikings	___	___/___
eek 4	Sun, Sep 29	1:00 PM	at Indianapolis Colts	___	___/___
eek 5	Sun, Oct 6	1:00 PM	Chicago Bears	___	___/___
eek 6	BYE WEEK				
eek 7	Sun, Oct 20	1:00 PM	at Green Bay Packers	___	___/___
eek 8	Sun, Oct 27	1:00 PM	at Houston Texans	___	___/___
eek 9	Sun, Nov 3	4:05 PM	Detroit Lions	___	___/___
eek 10	**Thu, Nov 7**	**8:20 PM**	**Los Angeles Chargers**	___	___/___
eek 11	Sun, Nov 17	4:25 PM	Cincinnati Bengals	___	___/___
eek 12	Sun, Nov 24	1:00 PM	at New York Jets	___	___/___
eek 13	**Sun, Dec 1**	**1:00 PM**	**at Kansas City Chiefs**	___	___/___
eek 14	Sun, Dec 8	4:25 PM	Tennessee Titans	___	___/___
eek 15	Sun, Dec 15	4:05 PM	Jacksonville Jaguars	___	___/___
eek 16	**Sun, Dec 22**	**1:00 PM**	**at Los Angeles Chargers**	___	___/___
eek 17	**Sun, Dec 29**	**4:25 PM**	**at Denver Broncos**	___	___/___

END OF SEASON RECORD:___/___

DIVISION TOTAL WIN/LOSS: ___/___

PHILADELPHIA EAGLES

Head Coach: Doug Pederson | 2018 Record: 9-7
First Round Draft Pick: Andre Dillard – T (22)

Wentz was hurt — again — so Nick Foles rode to the rescue — again. It was uncanny and impressive, taking the Eagles back to the playoffs after their stunning Super Bowl victory a year earlier, and even winning their Wild Card game, before falling to the Saints in the divisional round. But now Nick is gone. And it's time for the Carson Wentz act with no safety net. Which is one reason we love the move up in the draft to grab Tackle Andre Dillard — Carson Wentz simply cannot get beat up again. We also like the signing of Malik Jackson, making a strong defense even stronger — and welcome back, DeSean Jackson. The Eagles have plenty of talent — and fans are hoping that Pederson and Wentz are on their way to becoming a classic winning duo, and won't suffer from the "curse" of early success.

PHILADELPHIA EAGLES

TEAM SCHEDULE
Philadelphia Eagles

				W/L	RUNNING TOTAL
ep track of wins and losses (division games in bold)					
eek 1	**Sun, Sep 8**	**1:00 PM**	**Washington Redskins**	___	___/___
eek 2	Sun, Sep 15	8:20 PM	at Atlanta Falcons	___	___/___
eek 3	Sun, Sep 22	1:00 PM	Detroit Lions	___	___/___
eek 4	Thu, Sep 26	8:20 PM	at Green Bay Packers	___	___/___
eek 5	Sun, Oct 6	1:00 PM	New York Jets	___	___/___
eek 6	Sun, Oct 13	1:00 PM	at Minnesota Vikings	___	___/___
eek 7	**Sun, Oct 20**	**8:20 PM**	**at Dallas Cowboys**	___	___/___
eek 8	Sun, Oct 27	1:00 PM	at Buffalo Bills	___	___/___
eek 9	Sun, Nov 3	1:00 PM	Chicago Bears	___	___/___
eek 10	BYE WEEK				
eek 11	Sun, Nov 17	4:25 PM	New England Patriots	___	___/___
eek 12	Sun, Nov 24	8:20 PM	Seattle Seahawks	___	___/___
eek 13	Sun, Dec 1	1:00 PM	at Miami Dolphins	___	___/___
eek 14	**Mon, Dec 9**	**8:15 PM**	**New York Giants**	___	___/___
eek 15	**Sun, Dec 15**	**1:00 PM**	**at Washington Redskins**	___	___/___
eek 16	**Sun, Dec 22**	**4:25 PM**	**Dallas Cowboys**	___	___/___
eek 17	**Sun, Dec 29**	**1:00 PM**	**at New York Giants**	___	___/___

END OF SEASON RECORD:___/___

DIVISION TOTAL WIN/LOSS: ___/___

PITTSBURGH STEELERS

Head Coach: Mike Tomlin | 2018 Record: 9-6-1
First Round Draft Pick: Devin Bush – LB (10)

Can you say: dysfunctional? The Killer B's were supposed to deliver a Super Bowl; instead, Ben, Brown and Bell spent more time feuding and fussing than winning. Big Ben threw for more yards (5,129) than anyone else in the league, but the team wasn't good enough, and the Steelers missed the playoffs for the first time in five years. We've been fans of Coach Tomlin for years, but we were not fans of what went on in the Pittsburgh locker room last season. What once looked like an unbeatable combo is now chalked up to a huge missed opportunity, and the Steelers enter 2019 with JuJu Smith-Schuster and James Conner in line to take over for Brown and Bell. We like both, but the Steelers have tough competition from both Baltimore and Cleveland (yes, Cleveland), so the pressure is on Ben to bring this team together and win more than 9 games in 2019.

PITTSBURGH STEELERS

TEAM SCHEDULE
Pittsburgh Steelers

				RUNNING
...ep track of wins and losses *(division games in bold)*			W/L	TOTAL
...eek 1	Sun, Sep 8	8:20 PM	at New England Patriots	___ ___/___
...eek 2	Sun, Sep 15	1:00 PM	Seattle Seahawks	___ ___/___
...eek 3	Sun, Sep 22	4:25 PM	at San Francisco 49ers	___ ___/___
...eek 4	**Mon, Sep 30**	**8:15 PM**	**Cincinnati Bengals**	___ ___/___
...eek 5	**Sun, Oct 6**	**1:00 PM**	**Baltimore Ravens**	___ ___/___
...eek 6	Sun, Oct 13	8:20 PM	at Los Angeles Chargers	___ ___/___
...eek 7	BYE WEEK			
...eek 8	Mon, Oct 28	8:15 PM	Miami Dolphins	___ ___/___
...eek 9	Sun, Nov 3	1:00 PM	Indianapolis Colts	___ ___/___
...eek 10	Sun, Nov 10	4:25 PM	Los Angeles Rams	___ ___/___
...eek 11	**Thu, Nov 14**	**8:20 PM**	**at Cleveland Browns**	___ ___/___
...eek 12	**Sun, Nov 24**	**1:00 PM**	**at Cincinnati Bengals**	___ ___/___
...eek 13	**Sun, Dec 1**	**4:25 PM**	**Cleveland Browns**	___ ___/___
...eek 14	Sun, Dec 8	4:25 PM	at Arizona Cardinals	___ ___/___
...eek 15	Sun, Dec 15	1:00 PM	Buffalo Bills	___ ___/___
...eek 16	Sun, Dec 22	1:00 PM	at New York Jets	___ ___/___
...eek 17	**Sun, Dec 29**	**1:00 PM**	**at Baltimore Ravens**	___ ___/___

END OF SEASON RECORD:___/___

DIVISION TOTAL WIN/LOSS: ___/___

SAN FRANCISCO 49'ERS

Head Coach: Kyle Shanahan | 2018 Record: 4-12
First Round Draft Pick: Nick Bosa – DE (2)

The year started with such high hopes but before they could even get going, Jimmy Garoppolo suffered a season-ending injury, and there was really no chance for Shanahan's 49ers to do much of anything. It wasn't just the offense that sputtered. Consider this stat: the best team in the league had 27 interceptions last year; San Francisco had 2. *All year*. So, hit the rest button and start again: Garoppolo is healthy, Shanahan is still a quarterback coaching genius, and San Fran got the best defensive player in the draft by picking Nick Bosa at #2. We love tight end George Kittle (who doesn't love a 5th round draft pick who sets *the all-time record* for receiving yards by a tight end in a single season?). We're also excited about two defensive players drafted in the last three years: DeForest Buckner and Mike McGlinchey. Adding WR Jordan Matthews and RB Tevin Coleman should add more horsepower to the offense, and overall we expect the Niners to win more games in 2019– but they still have to deal with the Rams and the Seahawks, who have far more experience at winning recently.

SAN FRANCISCO 49'ERS

TEAM SCHEDULE
San Francisco 49'ers

ep track of wins and losses (division games in bold)

				W/L	RUNNING TOTAL
eek 1	Sun, Sep 8	4:25 PM	at Tampa Bay Buccaneers	___	___/___
eek 2	Sun, Sep 15	1:00 PM	at Cincinnati Bengals	___	___/___
eek 3	Sun, Sep 22	4:25 PM	Pittsburgh Steelers	___	___/___
eek 4	BYE WEEK				
eek 5	Mon, Oct 7	8:15 PM	Cleveland Browns	___	___/___
eek 6	**Sun, Oct 13**	**4:05 PM**	**at Los Angeles Rams**	___	___/___
eek 7	Sun, Oct 20	1:00 PM	at Washington Redskins	___	___/___
eek 8	Sun, Oct 27	4:05 PM	Carolina Panthers	___	___/___
eek 9	**Thu, Oct 31**	**8:20 PM**	**at Arizona Cardinals**	___	___/___
eek 10	**Mon, Nov 11**	**8:15 PM**	**Seattle Seahawks**	___	___/___
eek 11	**Sun, Nov 17**	**4:05 PM**	**Arizona Cardinals**	___	___/___
eek 12	Sun, Nov 24	4:25 PM	Green Bay Packers	___	___/___
eek 13	Sun, Dec 1	1:00 PM	at Baltimore Ravens	___	___/___
eek 14	Sun, Dec 8	1:00 PM	at New Orleans Saints	___	___/___
eek 15	Sun, Dec 15	4:25 PM	Atlanta Falcons	___	___/___
eek 16	**Sun, Dec 22**	**1:00 PM**	**Los Angeles Rams**	___	___/___
eek 17	**Sun, Dec 29**	**4:25 PM**	**at Seattle Seahawks**	___	___/___

END OF SEASON RECORD:___/___

DIVISION TOTAL WIN/LOSS: ___/___

SEATTLE SEAHAWKS

Head Coach: Pete Carroll | 2018 Record: 10-6

First Round Draft Pick: L.J. Collier – DE (29)

We think Russell Wilson is a top-five quarterback, but at some point, you can't continue to lose all the talent around you and keep winning. (Unless you're New England.) Kam Chancellor? Gone. Earl Thomas? Gone. Doug Baldwin? Gone. Remember Richard Sherman? Long gone. Pete Carroll has been amazing, perhaps the best in the league, at getting pro-bowl play from his late round picks, but even he will be challenged this year. Still, we love Wilson's ability to make plays and win games — just be prepared for all the highlights and big plays to feature names you have never heard of. We guess that's OK, winning is winning, and we still expect a winning season from the Seahawks.

SEATTLE SEAHAWKS

TEAM SCHEDULE
Seattle Seahawks

ep track of wins and losses *(division games in bold)*

				W/L	RUNNING TOTAL
eek 1	Sun, Sep 8	4:05 PM	Cincinnati Bengals	___	___/___
eek 2	Sun, Sep 15	1:00 PM	at Pittsburgh Steelers	___	___/___
eek 3	Sun, Sep 22	4:25 PM	New Orleans Saints	___	___/___
eek 4	**Sun, Sep 29**	**4:05 PM**	**at Arizona Cardinals**	___	___/___
Week 5	**Thu, Oct 3**	**8:20 PM**	**Los Angeles Rams**	___	___/___
eek 6	Sun, Oct 13	1:00 PM	at Cleveland Browns	___	___/___
eek 7	Sun, Oct 20	4:25 PM	Baltimore Ravens	___	___/___
eek 8	Sun, Oct 27	1:00 PM	at Atlanta Falcons	___	___/___
eek 9	Sun, Nov 3	4:05 PM	Tampa Bay Buccaneers	___	___/___
eek 10	**Mon, Nov 11**	**8:15 PM**	**at San Francisco 49ers**	___	___/___
eek 11	BYE WEEK				
eek 12	Sun, Nov 24	8:20 PM	at Philadelphia Eagles	___	___/___
eek 13	Mon, Dec 2	8:15 PM	Minnesota Vikings	___	___/___
Week 14	**Sun, Dec 8**	**8:20 PM**	**at Los Angeles Rams**	___	___/___
eek 15	Sun, Dec 15	1:00 PM	at Carolina Panthers	___	___/___
eek 16	**Sun, Dec 22**	**4:25 PM**	**Arizona Cardinals**	___	___/___
eek 17	**Sun, Dec 29**	**4:25 PM**	**San Francisco 49ers**	___	___/___

END OF SEASON RECORD:___/___

DIVISION TOTAL WIN/LOSS: ___/___

TAMPA BAY BUCCANEERS

Head Coach: Bruce Arians* | 2018 Record: 5-11
First Round Draft Pick: Devin White – LB (5)

*new coa

Maybe you saw this coming, but we didn't expect to see Bruce Arians back in the NFL, certainly not in the grueling job of head coach. It's not that we doubt his ability, but we are worried about his health. Nevertheless, if Bucs fans are hoping that Jameis Winston is in fact their franchise QB, Arians is a great bet to make that happen. Incredibly, Tampa Bay gained more yards per game than any other team in the NFL last year (we would have lost *that* bet), and Mike Evans was a top five receiver — but the defense just could not stop opponents, leading to a five-win season, and the firing of head coach Dirk Koetter. We're hoping Winston makes it, and we believe he has the talent to do so. Meanwhile, we love Tampa Bay's first round pick, Linebacker Devin White, who should help the Bucs bolster what was a truly poor defense in 2018. But this is Winston's year to put up or shut up. If he can clean up his play and lead his team, he could be the long-term key to Tampa Bay's quest for a return to the play-offs, something Bucs' fans have been yearning for a very long time.

TAMPA BAY BUCCANEERS

TEAM SCHEDULE
Tampa Bay Buccaneers

				W/L	RUNNING TOTAL
ep track of wins and losses *(division games in bold)*					
eek 1	Sun, Sep 8	4:25 PM	San Francisco 49ers	___	___/___
eek 2	**Thu, Sep 12**	**8:20 PM**	**at Carolina Panthers**	___	___/___
eek 3	Sun, Sep 22	4:05 PM	New York Giants	___	___/___
eek 4	Sun, Sep 29	4:05 PM	at Los Angeles Rams	___	___/___
eek 5	**Sun, Oct 6**	**1:00 PM**	**at New Orleans Saints**	___	___/___
eek 6	**Sun, Oct 13**	**9:30 AM**	**Carolina Panthers**	___	___/___
eek 7	BYE WEEK				
eek 8	Sun, Oct 27	1:00 PM	at Tennessee Titans	___	___/___
eek 9	Sun, Nov 3	4:05 PM	at Seattle Seahawks	___	___/___
eek 10	Sun, Nov 10	1:00 PM	Arizona Cardinals	___	___/___
eek 11	**Sun, Nov 17**	**1:00 PM**	**New Orleans Saints**	___	___/___
eek 12	**Sun, Nov 24**	**1:00 PM**	**at Atlanta Falcons**	___	___/___
eek 13	Sun, Dec 1	1:00 PM	at Jacksonville Jaguars	___	___/___
eek 14	Sun, Dec 8	1:00 PM	Indianapolis Colts	___	___/___
eek 15	Sun, Dec 15	1:00 PM	at Detroit Lions	___	___/___
eek 16	Sun, Dec 22	1:00 PM	Houston Texans	___	___/___
eek 17	**Sun, Dec 29**	**1:00 PM**	**Atlanta Falcons**	___	___/___

END OF SEASON RECORD:___/___

DIVISION TOTAL WIN/LOSS: ___/___

TENNESSEE TITANS
Head Coach: Mike Vrabel | 2018 Record: 9-7
First Round Draft Pick: Jeffrey Simmons – DT (19)

We said it last year, and we'll say it again: is Mariota great, or just good? Titans fans are asking the same question — and demanding answers from Head Coach Mike Vrabel if he expects to keep his job. With a bottom-five performance in yards per game and touchdowns, the Titans' offense didn't inspire much confidence in 2018. The only bright spot was running back Derrick Henry, and we are excited to see him continue to grow in 2019. The Titans also took a gamble in the draft — picking Jeffrey Simmons at the #19 spot. Experts had Simmons as a top 10 pick, but that was before he tore his ACL in college; now, he may not even play his rookie year. We know this has worked before (see Jaylon Smith, Dallas), but the Titans need help now, and they probably won't get much from Simmons in 2019.

TENNESSEE TITANS

TEAM SCHEDULE
Tennessee Titans

ep track of wins and losses *(division games in bold)*				W/L	RUNNING TOTAL
eek 1	Sun, Sep 8	1:00 PM	at Cleveland Browns	___	___/___
eek 2	**Sun, Sep 15**	**1:00 PM**	**Indianapolis Colts**	___	___/___
eek 3	**Thu, Sep 19**	**8:20 PM**	**at Jacksonville Jaguars**	___	___/___
eek 4	Sun, Sep 29	1:00 PM	at Atlanta Falcons	___	___/___
eek 5	Sun, Oct 6	1:00 PM	Buffalo Bills	___	___/___
eek 6	Sun, Oct 13	4:25 PM	at Denver Broncos	___	___/___
eek 7	Sun, Oct 20	4:05 PM	Los Angeles Chargers	___	___/___
eek 8	Sun, Oct 27	1:00 PM	Tampa Bay Buccaneers	___	___/___
eek 9	Sun, Nov 3	1:00 PM	at Carolina Panthers	___	___/___
eek 10	Sun, Nov 10	1:00 PM	Kansas City Chiefs	___	___/___
eek 11	BYE WEEK				
eek 12	**Sun, Nov 24**	**4:05 PM**	**Jacksonville Jaguars**	___	___/___
eek 13	**Sun, Dec 1**	**1:00 PM**	**at Indianapolis Colts**	___	___/___
eek 14	Sun, Dec 8	4:25 PM	at Oakland Raiders	___	___/___
eek 15	**Sun, Dec 15**	**1:00 PM**	**Houston Texans**	___	___/___
eek 16	Sun, Dec 22	1:00 PM	New Orleans Saints	___	___/___
eek 17	**Sun, Dec 29**	**1:00 PM**	**at Houston Texans**	___	___/___

END OF SEASON RECORD:___/___

DIVISION TOTAL WIN/LOSS: ___/___

WASHINGTON REDSKINS

Head Coach: Jay Gruden | 2018 Record: 7-9

First Round Draft Picks: Dwayne Haskins – QB (15); Montez Sweat – DE (26

It was just freaky. 33 years *to the day* after Redskins QB Joe Theisman suffered a gruesome compound fracture of his leg that ended his career, Redskins QB Alex Smith suffered almost the exact same injury, as Joe Theisman watched in horror from the stands. Whether or not Smith will ever play football again is an open question, but the question facing Washington now is: who will their starting quarterback be? They sure didn't have a good answer in 2018, after Smith went out. So, we love the fact that the Redskins drafted a quarterback, and we really love their choice of quarterbacks in Dwayne Haskins. Plus, they didn't have to trade up to get him, he fell all the way to #15, and will likely win the starting job. Washington also grabbed an excellent defensive end by trading back up into the first round to take Montez Sweat at #26. Add those rookies to some very impressive young players in years two and three — not to mention the ageless Adrian Peterson, who gained over 1,000 yards last year — and we like the way Washington will enter 2019.

WASHINGTON REDSKINS

Washington Redskins

				W/L	RUNNING TOTAL
ep track of wins and losses (division games in bold)					
eek 1	Sun, Sep 8	1:00 PM	at Philadelphia Eagles	___	___/___
eek 2	Sun, Sep 15	1:00 PM	Dallas Cowboys	___	___/___
eek 3	Mon, Sep 23	8:15 PM	Chicago Bears	___	___/___
eek 4	Sun, Sep 29	1:00 PM	at New York Giants	___	___/___
eek 5	Sun, Oct 6	1:00 PM	New England Patriots	___	___/___
eek 6	Sun, Oct 13	1:00 PM	at Miami Dolphins	___	___/___
eek 7	Sun, Oct 20	1:00 PM	San Francisco 49ers	___	___/___
eek 8	Thu, Oct 24	8:20 PM	at Minnesota Vikings	___	___/___
eek 9	Sun, Nov 3	1:00 PM	at Buffalo Bills	___	___/___
eek 10	BYE WEEK				
eek 11	Sun, Nov 17	1:00 PM	New York Jets	___	___/___
eek 12	Sun, Nov 24	1:00 PM	Detroit Lions	___	___/___
eek 13	Sun, Dec 1	1:00 PM	at Carolina Panthers	___	___/___
eek 14	Sun, Dec 8	1:00 PM	at Green Bay Packers	___	___/___
eek 15	Sun, Dec 15	1:00 PM	Philadelphia Eagles	___	___/___
eek 16	Sun, Dec 22	1:00 PM	New York Giants	___	___/___
eek 17	Sun, Dec 29	1:00 PM	at Dallas Cowboys	___	___/___

END OF SEASON RECORD:___/___

DIVISION TOTAL WIN/LOSS: ___/___

Scorecard

Keep Track Of Your Weekly Results

How'd you do? Use this sheet to keep track of your own score each week.

	Wins	Losses	Your Net Sco
Week 1	——	——	——
Week 2	——	——	——
Week 3	——	——	——
Week 4	——	——	——
Week 5	——	——	——
Week 6	——	——	——
Week 7	——	——	——
Week 8	——	——	——
Week 9	——	——	——
Week 10	——	——	——
Week 11	——	——	——
Week 12	——	——	——
Week 13	——	——	——
Week 14	——	——	——
Week 15	——	——	——
Week 16	——	——	——
Week 17	——	——	——
		TOTAL SCORE:	——

Regular season finished? Time for the play-offs!

zona Cardinals Atlanta Falcons Baltimore Ravens Buffalo Bills Carolina Panthers Chicago Bears Cincinnati Bengals
veland Browns Dallas Cowboys Denver Broncos Detroit Lions Green Bay Packers Houston Texans Indianapolis
ts Jacksonville Jaguars Los Angeles Chargers Los Angeles Rams Kansas City Chiefs Miami Dolphins Minnesota
ings New England Patriots New Orleans Saints New York Giants New York Jets Oakland Raiders Philadelphia
gles Pittsburgh Steelers San Francisco 49'Ers Seattle Seahawks Tampa Bay Bucanneers Tennessee Titans
shington Redskins Arizona Cardinals Atlanta Falcons Baltimore Ravens Buffalo Bills Carolina Panthers Chicago
ars Cincinnati Bengals Cleveland Browns Dallas Cowboys Denver Broncos Detroit Lions Green Bay Packers
uston Texans Indianapolis Colts Jacksonville Jaguars Los Angeles Chargers Los Angeles Rams Kansas City Chiefs
ami Dolphins Minnesota Vikings New England Patriots New Orleans Saints New York Giants New York Jets
kland Raiders Philadelphia Eagles Pittsburgh Steelers San Francisco 49'Ers Seattle Seahawks Tampa Bay
canneers Tennessee Titans Washington Redskins Arizona Cardinals Atlanta Falcons Baltimore Ravens Buffalo Bills
rolina Panthers Chicago Bears Cincinnati Bengals Cleveland Browns Dallas Cowboys Denver Broncos Detroit
ns Green Bay Packers Houston Texans Indianapolis Colts Jacksonville Jaguars Los Angeles Chargers Los Angeles
ms Kansas City Chiefs Miami Dolphins Minnesota Vikings New England Patriots New Orleans Saints New York
nts New York Jets Oakland Raiders Philadelphia Eagles Pittsburgh Steelers San Francisco 49'Ers Seattle
ahawks Tampa Bay Bucanneers Tennessee Titans Washington Redskins Arizona Cardinals Atlanta Falcons
timore Ravens Buffalo Bills Carolina Panthers Chicago Bears Cincinnati Bengals Cleveland Browns Dallas
wboys Denver Broncos Detroit Lions Green Bay Packers Houston Texans Indianapolis Colts Jacksonville Jaguars
s Angeles Chargers Los Angeles Rams Kansas City Chiefs Miami Dolphins Minnesota Vikings New England Patriots
w Orleans Saints New York Giants New York Jets Oakland Raiders Philadelphia Eagles Pittsburgh Steelers San
ncisco 49'Ers Seattle Seahawks Tampa Bay Bucanneers Tennessee Titans Washington Redskins Arizona Cardinals
anta Falcons Baltimore Ravens Buffalo Bills Carolina Panthers Chicago Bears Cincinnati Bengals Cleveland
wns Dallas Cowboys Denver Broncos Detroit Lions Green Bay Packers Houston Texans Indianapolis Colts
cksonville Jaguars Los Angeles Chargers Los Angeles Rams Kansas City Chiefs Miami Dolphins Minnesota Vikings
w England Patriots New Orleans Saints New York Giants New York Jets Oakland Raiders Philadelphia Eagles
sburgh Steelers San Francisco 49'Ers Seattle Seahawks Tampa Bay Bucanneers Tennessee Titans Washington
dskins Arizona Cardinals Atlanta Falcons Baltimore Ravens Buffalo Bills Carolina Panthers Chicago Bears
cinnati Bengals Cleveland Browns Dallas Cowboys Denver Broncos Detroit Lions Green Bay Packers Houston
ans Indianapolis Colts Jacksonville Jaguars Los Angeles Chargers Los Angeles Rams Kansas City Chiefs Miami
phins Minnesota Vikings New England Patriots New Orleans Saints New York Giants New York Jets Oakland
ders Philadelphia Eagles Pittsburgh Steelers San Francisco 49'Ers Seattle Seahawks Tampa Bay Bucanneers
nnessee Titans Washington Redskins Arizona Cardinals Atlanta Falcons Baltimore Ravens Buffalo Bills Carolina
nthers Chicago Bears Cincinnati Bengals Cleveland Browns Dallas Cowboys Denver Broncos Detroit Lions Green
y Packers Houston Texans Indianapolis Colts Jacksonville Jaguars Los Angeles Chargers Los Angeles Rams
nsas City Chiefs Miami Dolphins Minnesota Vikings New England Patriots New Orleans Saints New York Giants
w York Jets Oakland Raiders Philadelphia Eagles Pittsburgh Steelers San Francisco 49'Ers Seattle Seahawks

PLAYOFFS!

roit Lions Green Bay Packers Hous   le Jaguars Los Angeles Chargers Los
geles Rams Kansas City Chiefs Mia   sota Vikings New England Patriots New Orleans Saints New
k Giants New York Jets Oakland Raiders Philadelphia Eagles Pittsburgh Steelers San Francisco 49'Ers Seattle
ahawks Tampa Bay Bucanneers Tennessee Titans Washington Redskins Arizona Cardinals Atlanta Falcons
timore Ravens Buffalo Bills Carolina Panthers Chicago Bears Cincinnati Bengals Cleveland Browns Dallas
wboys Denver Broncos Detroit Lions Green Bay Packers Houston Texans Indianapolis Colts Jacksonville Jaguars
s Angeles Chargers Los Angeles Rams Kansas City Chiefs Miami Dolphins Minnesota Vikings New England Patriots
w Orleans Saints New York Giants New York Jets Oakland Raiders Philadelphia Eagles Pittsburgh Steelers San
ncisco 49'Ers Seattle Seahawks Tampa Bay Bucanneers Tennessee Titans Washington Redskins Arizona Cardinals
anta Falcons Baltimore Ravens Buffalo Bills Carolina Panthers Chicago Bears Cincinnati Bengals Cleveland
wns Dallas Cowboys Denver Broncos Detroit Lions Green Bay Packers Houston Texans Indianapolis Colts
cksonville Jaguars Los Angeles Chargers Los Angeles Rams Kansas City Chiefs Miami Dolphins Minnesota Vikings
w England Patriots New Orleans Saints New York Giants New York Jets Oakland Raiders Philadelphia Eagles
sburgh Steelers San Francisco 49'Ers Seattle Seahawks Tampa Bay Bucanneers Tennessee Titans Washington
dskins Arizona Cardinals Atlanta Falcons Baltimore Ravens Buffalo Bills Carolina Panthers Chicago Bears
cinnati Bengals Cleveland Browns Dallas Cowboys Denver Broncos Detroit Lions Green Bay Packers Houston
ans Indianapolis Colts Jacksonville Jaguars Los Angeles Chargers Los Angeles Rams Kansas City Chiefs Miami
phins Minnesota Vikings New England Patriots New Orleans Saints New York Giants New York Jets Oakland
ders Philadelphia Eagles Pittsburgh Steelers San Francisco 49'Ers Seattle Seahawks Tampa Bay Bucanneers
nnessee Titans Washington Redskins Arizona Cardinals Atlanta Falcons Baltimore Ravens Buffalo Bills Carolina
thers Chicago Bears Cincinnati Bengals Cleveland Browns Dallas Cowboys Denver Broncos Detroit Lions Green
y Packers Houston Texans Indianapolis Colts Jacksonville Jaguars Los Angeles Chargers Los Angeles Rams
nsas City Chiefs Miami Dolphins Minnesota Vikings New England Patriots New Orleans Saints New York Giants New
k Giants New York Jets Oakland Raiders Philadelphia Eagles Pittsburgh Steelers San Francisco 49'Ers Seattle
ahawks Tampa Bay Bucanneers Tennessee Titans Washington Redskins Arizona Cardinals Atlanta Falcons
timore Ravens Buffalo Bills Carolina Panthers Chicago Bears Cincinnati Bengals Cleveland Browns Dallas
wboys Denver Broncos Detroit Lions Green Bay Packers Houston Texans Indianapolis Colts Jacksonville Jaguars
s Angeles Chargers Los Angeles Rams Kansas City Chiefs Miami Dolphins Minnesota Vikings New England Patriots
w Orleans Saints New York Giants New York Jets Oakland Raiders Philadelphia Eagles Pittsburgh Steelers San
ncisco 49'Ers Seattle Seahawks Tampa Bay Bucanneers Tennessee Titans Washington Redskins Arizona Cardinals
anta Falcons Baltimore Ravens Buffalo Bills Carolina Panthers Chicago Bears Cincinnati Bengals Cleveland
wns Dallas Cowboys Denver Broncos Detroit Lions Green Bay Packers Houston Texans Indianapolis Colts
cksonville Jaguars Los Angeles Chargers Los Angeles Rams Kansas City Chiefs Miami Dolphins Minnesota Vikings
w England Patriots New Orleans Saints New York Giants New York Jets Oakland Raiders Philadelphia Eagles

Final Standings at End of 2018 Regular Season
(division winners in bold, wild card teams in italics)

NFC NORTH

Chicago Bears 12-6
Minnesota Vikings 8-7-1
Green Bay Packers 6-9-1
Detroit Lions 6-10

NFC SOUTH

New Orleans Saints 13-3
Atlanta Falcons 7-9
Carolina Panthers 7-9
Tampa Bay Buccaneers 5-11

NFC EAST

Dallas Cowboys 10-6
Philadelphia Eagles 9-7
Washington Redskins 7-9
New York Giants 5-11

NFC WEST

LA Rams 13-3
Seattle Seahawks 10-6
San Francisco 49ers 4-12
Arizona Cardinals 3-13

AFC NORTH

Baltimore Ravens 10-6
Pittsburgh Steelers 9-6-1
Cleveland Browns 7-8-1
Cincinnati Bengals 6-10

AFC SOUTH

Houston Texans 11-5
Indianapolis Colts 10-6
Tennessee Titans 9-7
Jacksonville Jaguars 5-11

AFC EAST

New England Patriots 11-5
Miami Dolphins 7-9
Buffalo Bills 6-10
New York Jets 4-12

AFC WEST

Kansas City Chiefs 12-4
Los Angeles Chargers 12-4
Denver Broncos 6-10
Oakland Raiders 4-12

Division Winners 2019

Fill in the division winners and wild cards, now that the regular season is done. Compare this to the predictions you made at the start of the season (back on page 5).

FC

YOUR PREDICTIONS	ACTUAL WINNERS
North _____	North _____
South _____	South _____
East _____	East _____
West _____	West _____
Wild Card 1 _____	Wild Card 1 _____
Wild Card 2 _____	Wild Card 2 _____

FC

YOUR PREDICTIONS	ACTUAL WINNERS
North _____	North _____
South _____	South _____
East _____	East _____
West _____	West _____
Wild Card 1 _____	Wild Card 1 _____
Wild Card 2 _____	Wild Card 2 _____

How did you do?

Count up your winning guesses and enter the number here: _____
Maximum Possible Score: 12

2018 Playoff Results

(winners in bold/seeding in parentheses)

WILD CARD ROUND

NFC

(6) **Philadelphia Eagles 16** at
(3) Chicago Bears 15

(5) Seattle Seahawks 22 at
(4) **Dallas Cowboys 24**

AFC

(6) **Indianapolis Colts 21** at
(3) Houston Texans 7

(5) **Los Angeles Chargers 23** at
(4) Baltimore Ravens 17

DIVISIONAL ROUND

NFC

(6) Philadelphia Eagles 14 at
(1) **New Orleans Saints 20**

(4) Dallas Cowboys 22 at
(2) **Los Angeles Rams 30**

AFC

(6) Indianapolis Colts 13 at
(1) **Kansas City Chiefs 31**

(5) Los Angeles Chargers 28 at
(2) **New England Patriots 41**

CONFERENCE CHAMPIONSHIPS

NFC

Los Angeles Rams 26 at
New Orleans Saints 23

AFC

New England Patriots 37 at
Kansas City Chiefs 31

SUPER BOWL 52

New England Patriots 13 vs.
Los Angeles Rams 3

How the Playoff Match-Ups Work

ost of you probably already know this, but here's a quick refresher course, st in case! At the end of the regular season, twelve teams qualify for the ay-offs. In both the AFC and the NFC, there are four divisions. The team th the best record in each division goes to the play-offs, so there are ur first eight play-off teams — four from the NFC, four from the AFC. en there are two wild card teams from each conference — these are the o teams with the best records that didn't win their division. They can me from any division in the conference, even the same division.

So, now you have your twelve teams, six from the AFC, six from the FC. Four division champs and two wild cards from each conference. The ur division champs are seeded #1 - #4, based on their regular season cords, the two wild card teams are seeded #5 and #6, again based on eir records.

In the first week (wild card weekend), teams #1 and #2 in each nference get a bye. Meanwhile, the other eight teams are matched as follows: the #3 seed in each conference plays the #6 seed in that nference; the #4 seeds play the #5 seeds.

The second week of the play-offs (the divisional round) you still have ght teams left — the four that won their games in the wild-card weekend, d the four teams that got a bye in the previous week. Here's how those ght teams play: in each conference, the #1 seed (well rested after their eek off) plays the lowest seeded team still alive; while the #2 seed plays e other team left in their conference.

By week three (conference championship round), you just have four ams left — the winners of the previous weekend's four games. The two maining AFC teams face off; the two remaining NFC teams face off, all w vying to be AFC or NFC conference champions.

And finally, the AFC champs meet the NFC champs for the Super Bowl.

Sometimes a picture makes it easier, right? Turn the page to see how e match-ups worked last year. And then take a shot at predicting what ll happen in this year's playoffs!

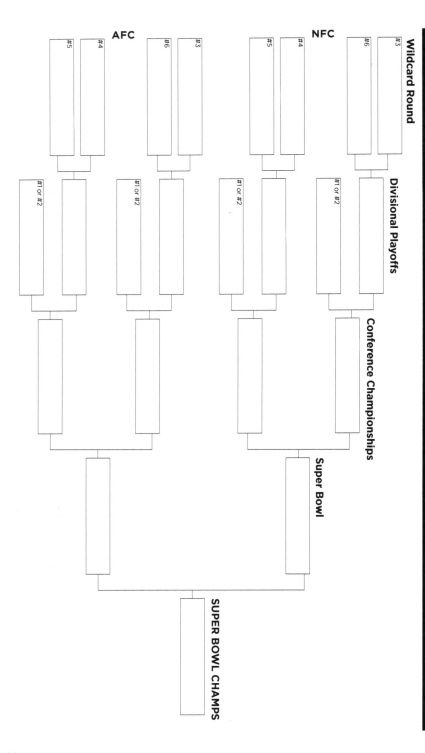

2019 Playoff Bracket Predictions
Fill In Your Picks at the Start of the Playoffs

Wildcard Round

Divisional Playoffs

Conference Championships

Super Bowl

SUPER BOWL CHAMPS

AFC

NFC

#3
#6
#4
#5

#3
#6
#4
#5

#1 or #2
#1 or #2
#1 or #2
#1 or #2

2019 Playoff Bracket Tracker
Keep Track of Playoff Results in Real Time

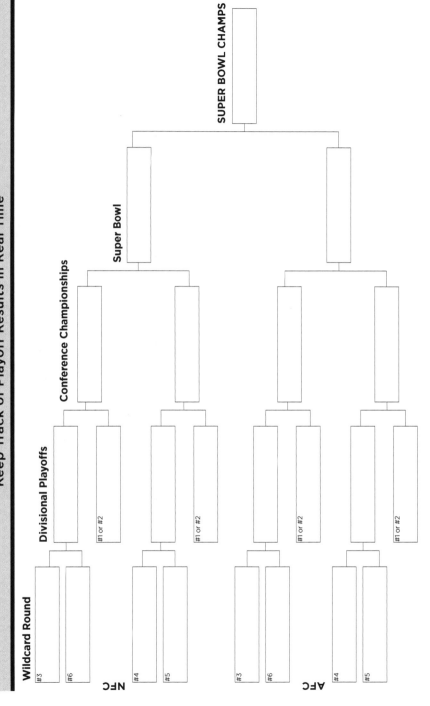

SUPER BOWL WINNERS (AND LOSERS) FROM 1967-2019

Super Bowl Winners and Losers

1967-2019

Year	Winner		Loser	
1967	Green Bay Packers	35	Kansas City Chiefs	1(
1968	Green Bay Packers	33	Oakland Raiders	14
1969	New York Jets	16	Baltimore Colts	7
1970	Kansas City Chiefs	23	Minnesota Vikings	7
1971	Baltimore Colts	16	Dallas Cowboys	1:
1972	Dallas Cowboys	24	Miami Dolphins	3
1973	Miami Dolphins	14	Washington Redskins	7
1974	Miami Dolphins	24	Minnesota Vikings	7
1975	Pittsburgh Steelers	16	Minnesota Vikings	6
1976	Pittsburgh Steelers	21	Dallas Cowboys	1;
1977	Oakland Raiders	32	Minnesota Vikings	14
1978	Dallas Cowboys	27	Denver Broncos	1(
1979	Pittsburgh Steelers	35	Dallas Cowboys	3
1980	Pittsburgh Steelers	31	Los Angeles Rams	1$
1981	Oakland Raiders	27	Philadelphia Eagles	1(
1982	San Francisco 49ers	26	Cincinnati Bengals	2
1983	Washington Redskins	27	Miami Dolphins	1;
1984	Los Angeles Raiders	38	Washington Redskins	9
1985	San Francisco 49ers	38	Miami Dolphins	1(
1986	Chicago Bears	46	New England Patriots	1(
1987	New York Giants	39	Denver Broncos	2(
1988	Washington Redskins	42	Denver Broncos	1(
1989	San Francisco 49ers	20	Cincinnati Bengals	1(
1990	San Francisco 49ers	55	Denver Broncos	1(
1990	San Francisco 49ers	55	Denver Broncos	1(

?ar	Winner		Loser	
91	New York Giants	20	Buffalo Bills	19
92	Washington Redskins	37	Buffalo Bills	24
93	Dallas Cowboys	52	Buffalo Bills	17
94	Dallas Cowboys	30	Buffalo Bills	13
95	San Francisco 49ers	49	San Diego Chargers	26
96	Dallas Cowboys	27	Pittsburgh Steelers	17
97	Green Bay Packers	35	New England Patriots	21
98	Denver Broncos	31	Green Bay Packers	24
99	Denver Broncos	34	Atlanta Falcons	19
)00	St. Louis Rams	23	Tennessee Titans	16
)01	Baltimore Ravens	34	New York Giants	7
)02	New England Patriots	20	St. Louis Rams	17
)03	Tampa Bay Buccaneers	48	Oakland Raiders	21
)04	New England Patriots	32	Carolina Panthers	29
)05	New England patriots	24	Philadelphia Eagles	29
)06	Pittsburgh Steelers	21	Seattle Seahawks	10
)07	Indianapolis Colts	29	Chicago Bears	17
)08	New York Giants	17	New England Patriots	14
)09	Pittsburgh Steelers	27	Arizona Cardinals	23
)10	New Orleans Saints	31	Indianapolis Colts	17
)11	Green Bay Packers	31	Pittsburgh Steelers	25
)12	New York Giants	21	New England Patriots	17
)13	Baltimore Ravens	34	San Francisco 49ers	31
)14	Seattle Seahawks	43	Denver Broncos	8
)15	New England Patriots	28	Seattle Seahawks	24
)16	Denver Broncos	24	Carolina Panthers	10
)17	New England Patriots	34	Atlanta Falcons	28
)18	Philadelphia Eagles	41	New England Patriots	33
)19	New England Patriots	13	Los Angeles Rams	3

Reserve Your Copy of the 2020 Edition of *Are You Ready for Some Football* now!

s the dog days of summer drag on and you pretend to care about baseball, ouldn't it be fun to start getting ready for the 2020 football season? Review our team's match-ups for the upcoming season, check out who's on tap r Thursday nights, Sunday nights, Monday nights, fill out your playoff redictions, and get ready for some football!

All you need to do is send me an email now at **MGRoss.Football@gmail.com**. ust let me know you might be interested in getting a copy of next year's uide. There's no commitment at all — except on my part: I will let you know s soon as the League releases its 2020 game schedules, and I will also let ou know when the 2020 guide will be ready for purchase.

It's an easy way to make sure you don't miss a thing. Because, if you are nything like me, you are ALWAYS ready for some football!

M.G.Ross
MGRoss.Football@gmail.com

68538239R00063

Made in the USA
Columbia, SC
08 August 2019